Mugged by
Mr. Badwrench

▼ ▼ ▼

Mugged by Mr. Badwrench

▼ ▼ ▼

An Insider's Guide to Surviving the
Shark-Infested Waters of Buying,
Maintaining, and Repairing Your Car

Sal Fariello

Illustrations by Bob Risch

St. Martin's Press   New York

Design by Judith Stagnitto

Library of Congress Cataloging-in-Publication Data

Fariello, Sal.
    [How to avoid getting mugged by Mr. Badwrench]
    Mugged by Mr. Badwrench : an insider's guide to surviving the shark-infested waters of buying, maintaining, and repairing your car / Sal Fariello.
       p.   cm.
    "A Thomas Dunne book."
    Reprint. Originally published: How to avoid getting mugged by Mr. Badwrench. Bay Shore, N.Y. : SFT Pub., 1988.
    ISBN 0-312-05474-2 (pbk.)
    1. Automobiles—Maintenance and repair.   2. Consumer protection—
    United States. I. Title.
    TL152.F335   1991
    629.28'72—dc20   90-19110
                               CIP

First Edition: April 1991

10 9 8 7 6 5 4 3 2 1

▼ ▼ ▼

Contents

Mugged by Mr. Badwrench

▼ ▼ ▼

1

▼ ▼ ▼

Naderism Is Dead

For consumers who are having trouble getting problems with their cars resolved, I've got some advice that will save you a lot of time, money, and aggravation—forget the "Sue the SOB's" doctrine preached for years by people such as Ralph Nader and his cohorts. There are better ways to solve your automotive problems than by going to court or by rushing into lemon-law proceedings.

This doesn't suggest that there aren't plenty of ruthless car dealers and dishonest repair shops ready to fleece you at the first opportunity. Like any other business, the automobile industry has its share of crooks. Abandoning the "Sue the SOB's" doctrine doesn't suggest that you should let yourself be intimidated by those crooks. It just means there are less expensive and less inconvenient methods of dealing with them than people like Ralph Nader would have you believe.

That may sound surprising to people who have grown to revere Nader as the champion of the downtrodden motorist, a reputation he garnered in part through his attacks in the 1960s on General Motors's Corvair, which he claimed was "unsafe at any speed." Actually, the Corvair was no less safe than any other small car of the day, a fact that was later substantiated by the Department of Transportation. In August 1972 the National Highway Traffic Safety Administration (NHTSA) sent a letter to owners of 1960–63 Corvairs. The letter said: "We have concluded that the handling and stability of the 1960–63 Corvair does not result in an abnormal potential for loss of control or rollover and that the handling and stability performance is at least as good as the performance of some other contemporary vehicles both foreign and domestic." The NHTSA's letter to Corvair owners also undermined the basis of Ralph Nader's allegations about the car's safety: "The GM test films which Mr. Nader alleged showed Corvairs being rolled over at speeds from 28 to 30 mph in fact showed that these vehicles were being deliberately rolled over by experienced test drivers for experimental purposes, and that they were developmental tests not representative of the practical driving environment. Such drivers could turn over other cars under similar developmental testing."

These conclusions arrived at by the NHTSA were based on extensive research and engineering studies including those done by the Texas A&M Research Foundation in 1971. The results of these studies were corroborated by a panel of three independent professional engineers hired by the NHTSA. The panel was composed of Ray Caldwell, President of Autodynamics Corporation; Edwin Resler, Jr., Ph.D., Director of the Graduate School of Aerospace Engineering at Cornell University; and Paul Wright, Ph.D., Associate Professor of Civil Engineering at Georgia Institute of Technology. These experts agreed that the NHTSA was correct and that Ralph Nader did not know what he was talking about—1960–63 Corvairs were safe and presented no greater hazards than Ford Falcons, Plymouth Valiants, Renaults or Volkswagens built during those years.

The Corvair, an economical, fuel-efficient small car, had been unjustifiably pummeled by Ralph Nader in his book *Unsafe at Any Speed*. The NHTSA attempted to set the record straight and calm the hysteria fomented by Nader. In NHTSA news release number 70–72 the Department of Transportation advised the media that Nader's allegations about the Corvair were false. But it was too late. The damage had already been done.

Unfortunately, by the time the truth came out the Corvair was virtually dead and Nader was thrust into the national consciousness as the righteous David who conquered the malevolent Goliath car company. All he really did was cause the extinction of an excellent economical car that was generally loved by its owners and is still loved by the many enthusiasts who belong to Corvair clubs across the country. Ironic, isn't it, that a fine automobile was killed by a man who, to this very day, doesn't even drive a car? But it did make Nader famous.

Once in the limelight, Nader had the ear of the American public, and his message suggested that the only way to keep auto manufacturers honest was to sue them. It was a message consumers believed, and it led to a tidal wave of litigation against car companies (and corporations in general) that swamped our legal system.

Nader's critics have questioned his motives for the belligerence he has shown against the auto industry in particular and many other industries as well. The implication is that he cares more about himself than about you, the consumer. Whatever his motives, what counts is whether or not the gospel of litigiousness he has preached really works. When it comes to the resolution of problems consumers have with their cars, the answer is no.

Essentially, Nader and the organizations he founded such as Public Citizen and the Center for Auto Safety have done nothing useful for the average motorist, nor are they likely to do so in the future. In the last twenty years there have been some remarkable advances made in automobile performance, quality, and safety. For the most part, you can thank Japanese competition for that, not Ralph Nader.

In the 1970s and early 1980s many of the models Detroit churned out were pure junk. Despite all the ranting and raving done by consumer advocates including Nader, Clarence Ditlow of the Center for Auto Safety, and Joan Claybrook (formerly with the National Highway Traffic Safety Administration and now with Public Citizen), despite all the lawsuits filed against carmakers, Detroit continued to build defect-ridden, unreliable automobiles. The consumer advocates had about as much effect on the quality of the cars rolling off Detroit's assembly lines as a gnat crashing into a windshield at 60 miles per hour.

The Japanese, however, were another story—more like Godzilla than a gnat! They flooded the American market with good quality, reliable cars built to standards that put Detroit to shame. Seeing their market share wither in the wake of the Japanese onslaught, Detroit finally got its act together and now builds many cars of quality equal to or better than those made in Japan. It was Japanese competition that finally got Detroit to wake up, not the rabble-rousing of a lot of anti-industry consumer crusaders.

Nevertheless, the self-styled saviors of the American motorist do not feel disenfranchised by the improvements made in American cars. Ever in search of an axe to grind with Detroit and carmakers in general, the crusaders continue to lobby our legislative bodies for "reforms" that supposedly benefit the average motorist. State lemon laws are examples of such reforms.

Because cars have become so technologically sophisticated, it's difficult to find anybody who knows how to fix them at any price. Often you have to put up with the frustration of returning to the repair shop over and over again to get the same problem resolved. And when the problem is with a new car that you expect to run properly, the frustration can be so great that you may be tempted to either buy a repair manual and fix it yourself, or take your complaints to court.

Lemon laws have been touted as a better option. Theoretically, they give you a cheap and simple alternative to the "Sue the SOB's" approach. All you have to do is go into arbitration (without a lawyer) and your grievance will be settled fairly. Consumers have been misled into believing that lemon laws are free; that the consumer crusaders have handed us something really wonderful on a silver platter. It's interesting how these people are so anxious to take credit for doing things for us they don't really do! They had nothing to do with giving us better-quality cars, and they haven't done anything to give us a no-cost way to resolve complaints about allegedly defective cars.

First, you must understand that lemon laws don't give you anything free. New York State, for example, which has a lemon law reputed to have real "teeth," belches out an endless stream of propaganda about how much the state's attorney general Robert Abrams has done to right the egregious wrongs the big bad car companies have done to so many New York drivers. In fact, Abrams's office has performed some useful services for motorists, but not for free. Not included in the state propaganda is the fact that New York car buyers pay more for their cars than buyers in other states. Some manufacturers place a surcharge of approximately $100 on each car sold in New York State to offset the enormous cost of red tape associated with dealing with New York's lemon laws.

Consumer advocates claim that only the manufacturers with the most consumer complaints are the ones that tack on the surcharge. Not true. Manufacturers that don't specifically assess an extra charge for cars sold in New York merely spread the added costs over the other forty-nine states. The point is, lemon laws do not give consumers anything free.

Ironically, lemon laws are largely unnecessary considering the competitiveness of the automotive marketplace. Once again, the Japanese have played a major role in indirectly coming to the aid of the consumer. There are too many new cars being manufactured and not enough customers to buy them. In this situation, the customer has clout. Manufacturers have to keep every customer they can, and they will go out of their way to accommodate a customer who has legitimate complaints and knows the proper way to voice them. This book will show you how to voice your complaints and negotiate a resolution so that you can stay out of court, out of arbitration, and out of the quagmire that so many lemon laws have created for consumers. More importantly, I'm going to show you ways to avoid getting into situations where you feel compelled to complain.

For many consumers this requires a readjustment in their beliefs. Consumer advocates such as Ralph Nader have convinced the American public that the car industry cannot be trusted; the people who *can* be trusted are the consumer advocates. Naturally they want you to believe that lemon laws and litigious resolution to car problems are best for you. Do you expect these people to admit that they are unnecessary and serve no useful function? Do you expect them to admit there is a better way to solve your problems, a simple way that will *prevent* you from having unresolved grievances about your car?

People like Ralph Nader seem to thrive on the faith of consumers in much the same way that television evangelists thrive on the adulation of true believers. Many television preachers have been exposed as being self-serving demagogues. Perhaps the day will soon come when consumers will begin to question the motives of consumer crusaders. Do these people really care about you and your problems with your cars, or do they have other objectives on their agenda? When you consider how they operate you may question whether they are just interested in making consumers dependent on them so they can feather their own nests.

Consider, for example, the issue of automotive safety. A group called Advocates for Highway and Auto Safety has been lobbying Congress to reduce the rural speed limit from 65 mph to 55 mph. This group also has been trying to force car manufacturers to equip all new cars with antilock brake systems. On the surface, it sounds like Advocates for Highway and Auto Safety really cares about the welfare of the American motorist. But let's look a little deeper.

The group's agenda is overseen by Clarence Ditlow, director of the Nader-founded Center for Auto Safety. Joan Claybrook, head of the Nader-founded Public Citizen group, is co-chairperson of Advocates for Highway and Auto Safety. And where is this organization getting its money? Along with Claybrook, the other co-chairperson is Gerald Maatman, president of Kemper National Property & Casualty Companies. Jack Trees, vice president and controller of Allstate Insurance Company, oversees the group's agenda along with Clarence Ditlow. Why the involvement of people from the insurance industry?

Their interest is quite simple. Insurance companies funded Advocates for Highway and Auto Safety to the tune of nearly a million dollars. Was this largess the result of the insurance industry's concern for driver safety? There have been insinuations made that they have been more concerned with getting Ralph Nader off their backs than with anything having to do with safety. As a result of pressure brought to bear by Ralph Nader in California, Proposition 103 was born, a referendum to reduce auto insurance and other insurance rates. This caused insurance companies no small amount of grief. It is interesting

that shortly thereafter, Nader-founded organizations
(Center for Auto Safety and Public Citizen) collaborated
with the insurance industry to harass auto manufacturers. Strange bedfellows, indeed! Not on the agenda of
Advocates for Highway and Auto Safety is the issue of
insurance rates.

But what about the matter of antilock brake systems
(ABS) and lower speed limits? Would these items represent a free gift from consumer advocates to the American
motorist? In fact, they would be no more free than lemon
laws, which promise to give consumers something for
nothing. Antilock brake systems cost nearly a thousand
dollars per car. Furthermore, they are more difficult to
diagnose and repair than conventional brake systems and
will increase the cost of maintenance over the life of a car
equipped with ABS. You pay more when you buy the car,
and you continue paying more to maintain the car. But
does added safety make it worth the money?

There is no evidence that ABS will prevent a significant
number of accidents. In fact, the opposite could occur.
Many marginally capable drivers could be lulled into a
false sense of security, believing that antilock brakes will
make their cars stop "on a dime" under all conditions.
Since antilock brakes are no panacea for sloppy driving
habits, many incompetent drivers could have more accidents because of a misplaced faith in the capabilities of
ABS systems. Accidents are usually caused by driver errors, not mechanical flaws in automobiles.

What about lowering the rural 65-mph speed limit? Will
this make our highways safer and save lives? The interstate highway system was designed so that cars could
safely negotiate *curves* in the highway at 80 mph. These
highways are designed *for speed!*

Critics of the 65-mph limit charge that accidents have
increased in areas where the limit has been raised. This is
just a manipulation of statistics. Thanks to the higher

speed limit, more people have been willing to travel by car according to data compiled by Citizens for Rational Traffic Laws. Because there has been an 8 percent increase in travel on rural interstate highways there has been a slight increase in accidents. In other words, there are more accidents because there are more cars on the road, not because the cars are being driven faster.

Furthermore, the occupancy rates per car affect accident data. Nobody really knows what the occupancy per car is, except that it has probably gone up due to an increase in automobile use for vacations and tourism. Therefore, claims that more people are getting injured in auto accidents because of higher speed limits are misleading. There may be more people in every car that is involved in an accident.

And finally, there is the matter of increased vehicle speed associated with the 55-mph versus 65-mph limit. In fact, the increase is not 10 mph. Average vehicle speed has gone up only about 3 mph because few people obey the 55-mph speed limit to begin with. So why has the insurance industry teamed up with various consumer groups to cram this unpopular traffic regulation down our throats?

The insurance industry would prefer that everybody buy very fast, expensive cars and never use them. Cars that are parked in driveways don't get into accidents. If speed laws make it impossible to enjoy a car trip or make automobile travel tediously slow, fewer people will use their cars. That translates into fewer accidents and damage claims and bigger profits for the insurance companies. Of course, since few people obey the 55-mph limit anyway, enforcing that unpopular limit will result in more traffic summonses being issued by the police and a wonderful excuse for insurance companies to raise rates for those people unlucky enough to get caught "speeding."

Do the insurance companies care about you? Don't bet on it. Do Ralph Nader-founded consumer organizations have your best interests at heart? Think twice before you assume that what they are up to will result in your getting anything for "free."

If you can't trust the people who claim to be your allies, just who can you trust? The answer is, yourself. If you are an informed consumer you don't need the Ralph Naders of this world, and to you Naderism will be a dead issue. This book will teach you how to protect your own interests so that you won't have to go through the expense of suing car dealers, auto manufacturers, and repair shops. You'll be shown how to avoid the maze of tedious legal codes, lemon laws, arbitration procedures and consumer groups all touted as the salvation of motorists who have been ripped off by automobile manufacturers and the automobile repair industry.

Instead, I'm going to show you how to get your car repaired painlessly in and out of warranty. Painlessly means no entanglements with lawyers, no involvement with arbitration procedures, and no need to get your knuckles busted trying to work on your car yourself.

I'll admit that litigation is in rare cases unavoidable when dealing with unscrupulous car dealers, dishonest repair shops or unresponsive auto manufacturers. But lawsuits, and to a lesser extent arbitration, make demands on your time and energy that can add to the hassles you have already experienced with your car.

Therefore, if you value your time, *preventing* the kinds of problems that necessitate legal action is a wise alternative. Instead of blindly walking into quicksand and turning to lawyers and consumer advocates to pull you out, it would be much more sensible for you to learn how to spot lousy car dealers and repair shops *before* you do business with them. It would also be sensible for you to learn enough about your car to know when it does need service and what a mechanic is talking about when he gives you a bill.

If you are unfortunate enough to have bought your car from a dealer with an inept service department and you're having trouble getting warranty work done, or if you think you're entitled to free repairs after your car's warranty has expired, there are ways to get what you want without resorting to arbitration or litigation. If you apply the suggestions given in this book, you'll have a good chance of happily staying on the road and out of court.

2
▼ ▼ ▼

The Cost of Getting Mugged

Buying a new car is usually a pleasant experience. Getting that new car fixed under warranty isn't. The friendly salesman who treated you like a VIP before you bought the car doesn't want to know you. Forget griping to the sales department—you'll only get the bum's rush there. So, on to the service department.

Ah, the service department. There you're greeted as though you were carrying a deadly plague. The guys in the shop just don't seem to take your complaints seriously. Or maybe they pretend to, but after a day in the shop your car still has the same problems. A few more tries at getting it fixed at the dealership and you're pretty well convinced you're barking up the wrong tree. So you write to the factory.

Welcome aboard the warranty merry-go-round. Next stop, the factory customer relations department. Your first letter gets no answer, so you write again. This time they respond, asking you to bring the car back to the lousy dealer who couldn't fix it in the first place. The factory representative is willing to look at your car. Now your hopes are up that this white knight from the factory will rescue you from the villains at the dealership. Your balloon gets popped fast when you see that this guy is just selling a bunch of platitudes. Dudes in three-piece suits don't fix cars, and this one isn't about to work on yours. But he'll give you his assurance that the next time the dealer will get the job done right. Sure!

After spending enough of your precious time spinning your wheels on the warranty treadmill, you give up, and resign yourself to the idea that your car is a lemon. So, you learn to live with the problems that seemed serious enough to deserve attention under the warranty. Too bad! Just after the warranty expires something goes *kaplunk* and the car stops running. Not forgetting the runaround you got from the dealer, you steer clear of their service department and opt for an independent shop.

Well, you got lumped by the dealer, bruised by the factory, and now you're ready to get mugged by some of the con men in the automotive aftermarket—the independent repair shops. There are some people in the aftermarket (that part of the industry not including the factories and their authorized dealers) who know you're not too thrilled with the service department at your car dealership, and that you're anxious for a good alternative. So, they're ready to take full advantage of your desperation. Letting your guard down for them is a big mistake.

According to a study done by the United States Department of Transportation as much as 40 percent of the money American consumers spend on auto repairs is wasted. Part of the waste is attributable to fraud. The rest is the result of incompetence—poor diagnosis and the replacement of expensive parts that have nothing wrong with them. The bottom line is that you stand an excellent chance of getting ripped off any time you bring your car in for service, whether at an independent shop or a dealer's service department.

Because of abuses motorists have endured in and out of warranty, many of them have grown to expect a raw deal from the automobile service industry. Complacently accepting that fate might have been a decision you could live with in the past, but with the rising prices of new cars, and repair parts and labor heading toward the stratosphere, how many of us can afford to give the auto industry a blank check? Unless you have money to burn, you're going to have to get serious about getting your money's worth out of your warranty, and *preventing* auto mechanics from picking your pockets. I emphasize "preventing" because avoiding getting gypped is a lot cheaper and less nerve-racking than trying to get your money back after it has happened.

And rest assured that some auto-repair people have a pretty big bag of tricks when it comes to separating unwary motorists from their money. Here are just a few of the ways they already may have taken you to the cleaners without your knowing it:

► After your car's warranty expired you paid for repairs for defective parts your dealer claimed were working "normally" while your vehicle was under warranty.

► You've paid for "tune-up" work that should have been done for free under your vehicle's five-year/50,000 miles emission controls warranty.

► You've paid for a new carburetor, fuel injectors, turbocharger, intake or exhaust manifold, or other parts that should have been covered under your vehicle's five-year/50,000 miles emission controls warranty.

► You've paid for costly brake overhauls when an inexpensive replacement of pads or linings would have sufficed.

► You've paid for a transmission tune-up your car did not require.

► You've paid for major automatic transmission work when minor service would have done just fine.

► You've paid a lot of money for air conditioner service that wasn't done.

► You've paid for wheel alignments your car didn't need.

► You've paid for shock absorbers, ball joints, or other steering parts that were not defective.

That's only a partial list. Later in this book we'll look at these and other repair scams in detail. The bottom line, though, is that if you're an average driver, you could easily get bilked out of a thousand dollars in needless or fraudulent repairs over the life of your vehicle. Wouldn't you rather blow that thousand bucks on a fun vacation in Acapulco instead of letting it slip into the greasy hands of Mr. Badwrench? Well, pack your bathing suit and suntan lotion! Because if you apply the secrets I'm going to tell you in this book, you should be able to block Mr. Badwrench's intrusions into your bank account and have the added bonus of a better-running car.

With the right tactics, there's no doubt that you can keep auto-repair con men from picking your pockets. Once they have your money, though, it's pretty hard to get it back. That's what most consumers fail to recognize. They make the mistake of thinking that manufacturer's representatives, arbitration panels, Better Business Bureaus, small claims courts, and government agencies will come to their rescue if they get gypped by a car dealer or independent repair shop. Mr. Badwrench counts on consumers to make these assumptions and exploits their gullibility to the maximum.

A lot of books have been written telling consumers how to use the legal system to redress their grievances against repair shops. All you have to do to implement the suggestions offered by some of these books is quit your job, become a lawyer, and have almost unlimited free time on your hands to get jerked around by the American system of justice. Even with the advent of state-legislated lemon laws, consumers have not always done too well. People who sit on arbitration panels have time to kill. Chances are you don't. So, even with arbitration available, relatively few disgruntled motorists are inclined to use it. And those who do, often are not too pleased with the results.

Well, what about small claims court? Sure, for a few bucks you can file a lawsuit without an expensive lawyer. And sure, after wasting countless hours of your time with adjournments and other stalling tactics the defense will use, you may get your fair hearing before a judge. And you may even win. But guess what? You may never collect a dime! Why? Because many small claims courts are so poorly funded that they don't have the resources to enforce payment from those who have lost their cases. That leaves you with a moral victory, but a broken car, and a depleted wallet. Score a victory for Mr. Badwrench.

Considering how tough it is for a consumer to get satisfaction after having been bilked by auto-repair gyp artists, it makes a lot more sense to follow a strategy that lowers the odds of getting ripped off. That's why the orientation of this book is toward prevention. In the long run it's cheaper, and it eliminates a lot of hassles. And who has the time for hassles these days? In almost every family both husband and wife have to work just to make ends meet. They have barely enough free time to go grocery shopping and cook dinner. So where do they find the time or the energy to pursue complex legal actions over their cars? Mr. Badwrench knows this. So he's pretty confident that when push comes to shove, the consumer will give up the fight out of frustration.

This doesn't mean that you can't intimidate Mr. Badwrench. It's just that the conventional ways of doing it often don't work too well. If you really want to intimidate the hell out of him, show him that you're not a complete bozo when it comes to the nuts and bolts of automobile repair. It's really important for you to avoid coming across as a chicken ready to be plucked when you deal with Mr. Badwrench, because the guy doesn't always have a lot of respect for you to begin with.

Have you ever gotten the feeling when talking to a repair-shop manager that you were being treated with disdain, as though you were some ignorant jerk because you didn't know anything about cars? Have you ever noticed one of these guys snickering at you like you were some dumb kid bellyaching about your petty little problems? Sometimes I've wondered if this condescending attitude also surfaces in some auto service advertisements. A case in point is a recent Meineke Muffler television ad campaign. In one group of commercials an assortment of misfits march into a muffler shop exclaiming: "I'm not going to pay a lot for this muffler and I want quality!" What's the point to these skits? Why are the motorists in Meineke commercials portrayed as half-witted caricatures instead of well-balanced, articulate adults? Is this the way the auto repair industry sees its customers? Unfortunately, some customers deserve derision. Any person who storms into a repair shop insisting on bargain-basement prices *and* top quality really does look and sound like a bonehead. And it's a customer like that who Mr. Badwrench loves to chisel the most. So avoid the tactic—it doesn't work.

Again, it's knowledge that impresses Mr. Badwrench, not the loudmouthed antics of an uninformed blowhard. Besides, any reasonable person knows that quality and low price are not often bedfellows. Expect to pay fair prices for good automotive work. There are some superb auto-repair technicians out there and they don't work cheap. This book will help you to find them and get your money's worth from them when you do.

3
▼ ▼ ▼

The Right Way to Choose a Dealer and Buy a Car

If a rock-bottom price is your only concern when you buy a new car you're bound to get burned! Yet many so-called experts tell consumers to buy their cars from whichever dealership offers the lowest selling price. That kind of advice comes from people who don't know anything about the car business and it often buys you a one-way ticket on the train to very expensive service nightmares.

As an example of the hogwash most consumers receive from "experts," consider something the much-publicized Jack Gillis (author of *The Car Book*) was quoted as saying according to an article in the February 12, 1989, *Seattle Times*. Asked by columnist Shelby Gilje whether consumers should buy at the dealership offering the lowest possible price even though there is no intention of having the car serviced there, Gillis said:

Yes, negotiate for the lowest price. Dealers are obligated to provide service under warranty regardless of where you bought the car. Some dealers will make it difficult if you don't buy from them, but don't sit still for this. You've got a warranty. Raise hell with the dealer. Bug the manufacturer's zone office or corporate headquarters, if necessary.

The columnist then asked Gillis if the consumer should ask to see the service department and meet the service manager when buying a new car. He was quoted as saying:

There is no correlation between sales and service . . . you are buying a car, not a dealership.

Gillis's uninformed, naïve comments are representative of the kind of misinformation being dumped on consumers by people who have limited direct experience in the automotive industry, have never worked for dealers or manufacturers, or haven't the vaguest idea of what really goes on in the car business. These days, when you buy a car, you *are* buying the dealership, for reasons we'll see later in this chapter.

Interestingly, Gillis has been closely allied with the Center for Auto Safety group, which finds itself embroiled in one way or another with an endless succession of lawsuits and adversarial petitions to the National Highway Traffic Safety Administration calling for aggressive government action against the auto industry. Gillis also has been closely connected with the insurance industry, which has shown considerable hostility toward car manufacturers and dealers.

It is, therefore, no surprise that Gillis would make comments that suggest the consumer adopt a confrontational posture toward car dealers and manufacturers. It would make a lot more sense for consumers to avoid situations where confrontations are likely to occur. The best way to do this is to be selective about where you buy a car. Not being selective about where you buy a car on the grounds that you can always get your car's warranty enforced in court makes as much sense as not being selective about who you marry because you can always get a divorce. Divorce lawyers just love people who reason that way! They create an endless need for the services of attorneys. Who needs the hassles?

Don't Jump at the Lowest Price!

Therefore, avoiding service hassles with your vehicle begins with buying it from the *right* dealership, not necessarily the one that offers the lowest selling price. It is nearly always worth it in the long run to spend a few hundred dollars more to buy a new car from a dealership with a conscientious service department. Now that may sound like heresy to people who have been indoctrinated by *Consumer Reports* magazine and other consumer publications, but I'm going to repeat it again: *It is nearly always worth it in the long run to spend a few hundred dollars more to buy a new car from a dealership with a conscientious service department.*

Why is the dealer so important, considering that you'll have a manufacturer's warranty? You have to realize that a new-vehicle warranty is really no better than the dealer's ability and willingness to honor it. Sure, the warranty is made by the manufacturer, not the dealer. But who actually fixes the cars? Ford, Chrysler, and General

Motors don't send mechanics from Detroit to repair cars do they? I haven't heard of any mechanics flying here from Japan to fix Toyotas, have you? The manufacturers just make the promises; the dealers have to fulfill them. And franchised dealers are independent businesspeople who cannot be controlled easily by the manufacturers. So, if you buy a car from a dealer with a second-rate service department, you'll get second-rate warranty work. That's why it's so important for you to know how to judge the service capabilities of a dealer before you buy a new car.

Consumer Reports's *Poppycock*

When it comes to cars, if you make the mistake of blindly following the half-truths and other rubbish disguised as money-saving tips in *Consumer Reports* magazine and some others like it you'll be doing yourself a big disservice. Here's why.

Consumer Reports makes much ado about the importance of getting the absolute lowest, rock-bottom price quote on your new car. They even offer a service (for a fee) that gives you a printout of the dealer's cost of a new car and every major option available on that car. Theoretically, once you know what the dealer's costs are, you can negotiate *up* from dealer-invoice cost instead of *down* from factory-sticker price. *Consumer Reports* would have their readers believe that all that counts is the bottom line—not *where* you buy the car, but which dealer gives you the *lowest price*.

Why is this advice shoddy? Surprisingly, the answer to this can be found within the pages of *Consumer Reports* itself. A revealing article entitled "New York to Ford: Shape Up!" can be found on page 211 in the April 1990 annual auto issue. The article tells the horror story of a Staten Island, New York, woman who bought a 1989 Ford Taurus from a dealership in Brooklyn. According to the article, the woman was told by the Brooklyn dealer that she could take her car to any Ford dealer on Staten Island for warranty repairs. To her chagrin, the woman found that two Ford dealers on Staten Island refused to perform warranty work, telling her to go back to Brooklyn where she bought the car. Later, she complained to the New York State Attorney General's office.

The article attributed the refusal of the Staten Island dealers to do warranty work to Ford's supposedly lax policy that limits warranty-repair obligations to the selling dealer in metropolitan areas where there are other Ford dealers. The *Consumer Reports* story went on to say that Ford is about to change this policy. Considering the title of the story and its hostile tone ("New York to Ford: Shape Up!") the implication is that Ford has done something wrong and will bow to pressure from the New York State Attorney General's office. This is an example typical of the way *Consumer Reports* attempts to boost its own stock by denigrating the auto industry using innuendo and half-truth.

Naturally *Consumer Reports* would run a story like this, because later in the same issue their editors spew out misinformation about buying a car from the lowest-priced dealer. What they are trying to do with this article is reinforce the fallacy that you can buy your car anywhere at the cheapest price and still get adequate protection under your warranty. It doesn't work that way! However, *Consumer Reports* would have their readers believe that manufacturers, Ford included, can be coerced into performing under warranty. Baloney! Dealers generally don't care about what Ford tells an attorney general, or what any manufacturer promises an attorney general. The simple fact of life in the car business is that, regardless of what the manufacturer agrees to, if the *dealer* doesn't want to fix your car you're generally screwed. Period. And that's true whether you buy a Ford or any other make of car.

That doesn't mean that a dealer would out-of-hand *refuse* to fix your car. There are other ways to torture a consumer, like making you wait a month for an appointment to get into the shop, or ordering the wrong parts so that your car is disabled a few weeks when it finally does get into the shop, and so on. Is *Consumer Reports* unaware of this? That would be surprising, because everybody in the automobile industry knows it's true.

So why don't they talk about it? Consider an article that ran in the same issue as the "New York to Ford: Shape Up!" story. Entitled "The Thompsons Buy a Taurus: How to Dodge $3,000 in Unnecessary Costs," the story tells the tale of a husband and wife who traveled 90 miles from their home in Payson, Arizona, to Phoenix to buy a new Ford because they didn't like the price quoted by the dealer in their hometown. Using a *Consumer Reports* new-car and used-car pricing printout, the Thompsons supposedly saved nearly $3,000 by buying their new car and trading in their old one in Phoenix. Of course, they had to pay hotel and travel bills, and presumably their time is worth something, so the savings were not quite so great. But when the Thompsons need warranty work from their local dealer in Payson, will they get the same bum's rush the Staten Island woman got? There's a good chance they will. Any local merchant is bound to resent a consumer who would travel so far to buy a product in preference to supporting the local economy.

And besides, did this couple really save $3,000? Not likely. The car business is so competitive these days that any good shopper can get a fine deal on a new car by haggling a bit. It is worth the effort to get an approximation of what a dealer pays the manufacturer for a car. This information is available from a variety of sources including *Edmund's* guides, which are sold in most bookstores. However, this knowledge does not guarantee the consumer that a dealer will sell a new car for 4 percent over cost as the *Consumer Reports* story implies. The minimum profit a dealer will accept is largely governed by supply and demand. If demand is high and you push for a deal three or four hundred dollars over cost you'll be thrown out of the showroom. Every merchant has a right to make a fair profit on merchandise.

Yet, if you believe the drivel you read in publications like *Consumer Reports*, it would appear that a dealer is committing a crime when he attempts to get list price for a car. Just what is so scandalous about getting list price for any piece of merchandise? If the consumer is not a good shopper, he's going to pay "full freight" as the saying goes, whether the purchase is a car, a television, or a toaster. On the other hand, a smart shopper easily can save money on a new car. Rarely though, do you have to travel a great distance to do it.

In the Thompson's case, while the dealer in Payson might not have been willing to match the price offered by the dealer in Phoenix, ultimately, he probably would have come very close. Even if he had demanded $500 more, it could have been worth it. The trip to Phoenix cost a bundle and required a lot of time. It could require a lot more time if the Thompsons are forced to return to Phoenix for warranty work.

Of course, *Consumer Reports* would have us believe a dealer can be coerced into doing warranty repairs. Like the disgruntled Staten Island car buyer, the Thompsons can always run to the state attorney general's office and complain if it comes to that. *Consumer Reports* apparently would have us believe that Big Brother will protect us all. That's a lot of nonsense. The best protection is a business that values its local customers.

However, people of the *Consumer Reports* ilk are of the opinion that the government should protect the consumer. When problems arise, litigate. Run to the attorney general's office—look to government to bail you out. This kind of mentality at *Consumer Reports* is not surprising. On their board of directors sits Clarence Ditlow of the Center for Auto Safety and Joan Claybrook of Public Citizen, both noted for their prodding for government intervention in consumer issues. If these people had any good advice for consumers when it comes to buying new cars, it would not be necessary to run to the government for redress of grievances because most of the grievances would not occur. The key is the dealership, not simply the lowest price of the new car.

It's unfortunate that so few consumers take the time to evaluate a dealership's service department before making a major investment in a new car. This is really ironic. A consumer with limited financial resources will usually plop down ten or twenty thousand bucks for a car without a second thought about the dealer's ability to service it. On the other hand, multibillion-dollar companies like Ford or General Motors wouldn't dream of spending that much money on a piece of equipment for a factory without being certain the manufacturer could support it with good service if it malfunctioned. In industry they're skeptical—but consumers go on believing sales hype and get rooked all the time.

A lot of people think they can have the best of both worlds by buying a car from a dealer known for low prices, and then having warranty work done at some other shop known for good service. You should avoid this self-delusion. A dealer who hasn't sold you a car won't go out of his way to help you with difficult warranty problems. And if you want to get all you're entitled to from the factory with minimal grief, you're definitely going to need your selling dealer's help. Remember, your objective has to be to *prevent* problems with auto-service people, instead of naïvely walking into quicksand and hoping that arbitration or litigation gets you out.

There are several ways a service-oriented selling dealer can help you avoid this inconvenience. Car dealers are not all equal in terms of their ability to negotiate concessions from the manufacturers they represent. Dealers with good service departments usually get more cooperation from manufacturers' service organizations than dealers known for generating a lot of customer complaints. When you need help with your car, the service manager in your selling dealership can exert substantial influence on the manufacturer to grant you concessions, assuming the service manager works for a dealership with a good service reputation. If you are seeking special help from a service manager whose dealership did not sell you the car, your entreaties will likely fall on deaf ears.

Additionally, many service managers have an internal budget called a *shop policy* account. This account makes funds available to the service manager for situations involving good customers who deserve special assistance. These funds are never spent on customers who bought their cars at some other dealership.

Maybe you think you don't need a service manager's intervention to get all you're entitled to under warranty. Perhaps you believe you can bargain with the manufacturer on your own behalf. In all my years in the car business I've seen some of the hardest bargaining, most self-assured tigers claw a great deal out of a salesman in the showroom only to become helpless sheep when they faced the service people in the shop. Ignorance of the politics that goes on back there between the dealership and the manufacturer could get you fleeced. Your best bet is to buy your car from a conscientious dealership that will go to bat for you against the factory when you need special warranty assistance.

Consequently, there's plenty of financial incentive to take the quality of a dealer's warranty service seriously before you buy a new car there. What you don't get free under warranty, you'll probably wind up paying for after the warranty expires. Besides, when you buy a new vehicle, you're paying for your warranty—it doesn't come free. The anticipated warranty costs per car are factored into the price the factory charges its dealers, and these costs are ultimately passed on to you. So why shouldn't you take advantage of something you have already paid for?

Unfortunately, many car dealers are normally not too anxious to do warranty work because there can be hassles getting the manufacturer to pay for it. It's fairly easy to dupe the average customer with a padded repair bill to cover the costs of a mechanic's mistakes. The manufacturer isn't so easily tricked. Auto manufacturers often refuse to pay dealers for parts and labor expenses when there is a suspicion of mechanic error. Furthermore, the paperwork necessary to file a warranty claim against the factory is time-consuming and costly. Especially costly is a rejected claim! When the customer is paying the bill, these problems don't arise.

So how do you make sure you're buying from a dealership that won't give you big problems with your warranty? I'll take it for granted that you've already heard all the standard suggestions about checking with your local Better Business Bureau, the consumer affairs department, and other similar agencies before you buy a car from a particular dealer. It's worth the effort, so go ahead and do it. And while you're at it, don't forget to ask your acquaintances about any knowledge they may have of the dealership you're considering. But don't stop there. Go a few steps beyond this and you'll get some objective insight into the kind of warranty service you could expect.

The Customer Satisfaction Index

To begin with, before you consider buying a car from a particular dealership, you should determine the dealership's *customer satisfaction index*, known in the auto industry as CSI. CSI is a rating assigned to the dealership by the manufacturer based on surveys of the dealership's customers. The surveys determine the level of customer satisfaction with the sales and service departments. Some very small volume dealerships might not have CSI ratings assigned to them for all makes they sell.

Because the ratings are assigned by the manufacturers, you might assume they are self-serving and inaccurate. Not so! In the fiercely competitive automotive marketplace, every customer counts. Manufacturers are now very sensitive to customer-relations problems created by their dealerships, so the surveys are designed to accumulate meaningful data. CSI ratings provide a good indication of what you can expect from a dealership in terms of customer service. There are plenty of dealerships with very poor ratings—you should not buy a car from one of these.

To find out what a dealership's CSI ratings are, ask the salesperson. Dealerships with good scores will be happy to show you what they are. Those with substandard scores will evade the issue. So that you can understand how to interpret CSI data, let's consider a CSI report that a typical General Motors dealership would show you. Other manufacturers use different report nomenclature but their reports contain essentially the same information. For example, Ford Motor Company has what they call the QC-P program. QC-P, which stands for Quality Commitment-Performance, is Ford's proprietary customer-satisfaction rating system. Unlike GM's system, which rates dealer performance in percentages up to 100 percent,

Ford's system assigns a point rating up to a maximum of 10 points.

The first page of a GM CSI report contains the title "Dealer Report of Customer Satisfaction" along with the issue date. Make sure the report you are shown is recent. The next page, labeled *A*, is titled "Key Measures of Customer Satisfaction." The following page, labeled *1*, is the page containing the data you need.

There are two columns on the page. Each column contains CSI average percentages; one column indicates the last twelve months and the other lists the percentages for the last three months. Basically, the three-month column reveals short-term trends in the dealership's performance. You should pay attention to the twelve-month CSI scores.

Overall Satisfaction with Selling Dealer

The only CSI score you have to worry about is called "Overall Satisfaction with Selling Dealer." There are three CSI scores listed for overall satisfaction. A separate overall satisfaction score is found in each of three columns which are labeled YOUR AVERAGE (meaning the dealer's average), ZONE AVERAGE, and DIVISION AVERAGE. The important numbers are the dealer's average (YOUR AVERAGE) *compared to* the zone average.

DIVISION AVERAGE refers to the *nationwide* performance of an entire division of the parent corporation, for example, Pontiac Division of General Motors Corporation or Buick Division and so forth. This number is meaningful to the manufacturer but not to the average customer. ZONE AVERAGE is important because it measures the performance of dealers in a *limited geographical area* or "zone." This figure tells you how other similar dealerships in your area are performing in terms of customer satisfaction.

YOUR AVERAGE is the dealership's absolute performance and must be compared to the zone average to be meaningful.

The dealership's absolute average by itself is not important. Suppose, for example, that a dealership has an overall satisfaction of 80 percent. If the zone average is 78 percent, the dealership score of 80 percent is quite good. On the other hand, if the zone average is 85 percent, the dealership's average of 80 percent is not good at all. *You should buy your car from a dealer whose overall CSI rating is at or above zone average.*

The reason a dealership's score *relative to the zone* is important is because high-zone customer satisfaction ratings are more difficult to achieve in some areas of the country. In the New York metropolitan area, for example, a zone average of 80 percent might be excellent, whereas in a rural zone in the Midwest 80 percent could be low. Consumers in the major metropolitan areas typically are harder to please than those in small towns. Also, small-town dealers generally take better care of their customers.

You should not let CSI ratings influence your decision about the car you want to buy. For example, suppose you want to purchase a Buick and discover that the zone CSI average is 80 percent. Then, you discover later on that the zone CSI rating for Oldsmobile is 85 percent. It would be a mistake to alter your decision and opt for an Oldsmobile because of the difference in zone CSI ratings. CSI ratings for a car line can be influenced by various demographic factors, including the age group of the people who typically buy a certain make of car. Age can affect product expectations and overall satisfaction. Therefore, you first should decide on the kind of car you want, then you should select a dealership with a good CSI score.

If you're lucky, you might locate a car dealership with truly exceptional CSI ratings, although they are few and far between. One GM dealership in Kendallville, Indiana,

Steve West Motors, has achieved some notability for their excellent customer service. With CSI ratings as high as 96 percent and well above zone average, this dealership is the kind from which a customer could safely buy a new car without worries about having nightmares getting warranty work done. Unfortunately, the whole country can't flock to Kendallville, Indiana, to buy a car. And not everybody wants to buy GM products.

J. D. Power Surveys

The fact that there are so many choices of new cars raises the question of why you shouldn't just buy the cars that are most highly rated in the J. D. Power quality surveys, which are heavily publicized in the media. Wouldn't this be a guaranteed way to avoid warranty hassles?

Absolutely not! The J. D. Power initial quality surveys indirectly suggest that what matters most in avoiding warranty and service hassles is the dealership, not the make of car. The reason for this is that virtually all cars built in the U. S., Japan, and Western Europe are now roughly equal in quality. According to the Power surveys, the difference between the average Asian-built car and the average U. S.-built car is one-half of a defect per car. In other words, the Japanese are, as of this writing, about one-half of a defect per car better than the domestic manufacturers. When was the last time you took your car to a dealership to have half of a defect repaired?

Even if a half-defect quality gap meant anything (which it doesn't), the gap is closing. Therefore, whether you buy American or choose an import, chances are you are going to get a car of approximately equal quality. What will vary in quality immensely, however, are the dealers that sell cars; and if you buy from the wrong one, regardless of the quality of the car, you could wind up with a lot of grief. So, let's look at some additional ways to judge a dealership before you make the decision to buy.

Service Excellence Awards

Nearly all car manufacturers issue special awards to dealerships that perform exceptionally well in terms of service to their customers. These awards are not given whimsically. Dealerships that don't earn them, don't get them.

In business there's an old adage that if you want to know what a prospective employee will do in the future, check out what he or she has done in the past. You could apply this logic to your selection of a car dealership. One that has won a service award in the past will probably give good service in the future.

Ask your salesperson if the dealership has won an award and ask to see it. If the award is recent, you have been fortunate to find a dealership a cut above the rest.

A Quick Test You Can Perform

Another way to screen out the good dealerships from the lemons involves a simple test. It gives you an idea as to how a dealership treats warranty-related complaints in comparison to those for which a customer would have to pay. Here's a test you can do.

Suppose you're thinking of buying a brand-new DreamMobile from ABC Motors. The first thing you need to find out is the length of DreamMobile's warranty and what it covers. Next, try calling ABC for a service appointment under a fictitious name, pretending that your car isn't running normally. Say that your automatic transmission is slipping and not shifting properly. Tell the service writer or scheduling clerk that you bought your car from ABC Motors just a few months ago, so it's definitely under warranty. Then, see how long you have to wait until they can look at your car. Don't actually make an appointment—just say you'll call back as soon as you check your calendar to see if you are free on the service date available.

A few minutes later, have a friend call ABC claiming to own a DreamMobile with a similar complaint that obviously cannot be covered under warranty. For example, if the warranty on automatic transmissions on Dream-Mobiles is four years or 40,000 miles, your friend should say the car has 50,000 miles on it. Also, your friend should say that the car was purchased from another dealership. Now, see how soon they are willing to take a look at your friend's car. If ABC Motors is like many dealerships, customer-paid labor gets priority over warranty work, even warranty work required on cars sold to their own customers. Consequently, a warranty repair might be delayed for weeks at their shop. You want to avoid such a dealership, or buy a lot of antacid tablets when you do buy your car there—your stomach will need them.

A word of caution here, however. The test I've just described should be repeated a few times over the course of a couple of weeks to establish a scheduling pattern. Each time, use a different fictitious malfunction, like a brake problem, an alternator problem (charge warning light on), or other mechanical trouble. Of course, make sure that there's no doubt you're calling about a vehicle under warranty, while your friend is clearly in need of customer-paid repairs. And don't actually book an appointment unless you call to cancel it an hour later. Otherwise, you might deprive some customer in real need of an appointment slot.

Checking Out a Service Department

There are things you can find out about a dealership by checking out its service department before you buy a car there. Ask any sweet-talking car salesman how his service department is. You'll probably get a look of righteous indignation that you could even doubt that his shop wasn't a model of technical excellence. Forget everything these guys tell you—they'll say anything to sell you a car.

Instead, pay a short visit to the shop. Look around. Does it look neat and organized? Do the mechanics look like filthy grease monkeys or are they attired in reasonably clean uniforms? If they're all slobs, the grease will wind up on your paint and upholstery. Furthermore, a slovenly attitude about outward appearance in a repair shop often betrays something negative about the work ethic. Is the shop well lighted? If the weather is cold, does the shop feel comfortably warm? Since you're not looking for a job there, you might think this doesn't affect you. Well, you may be wrong! Lousy working conditions (very common in the automobile industry) lead to slipshod work and high employee turnover.

In my experience working with manufacturers, turnover has been one of the leading causes of festering customer complaints about automobile dealer service departments. Here's why. You bring your car into the shop and spill your guts to the service manager about all the problems your car is giving you. He makes all kinds of promises about what will be done to the car to fix it. A few weeks later you bring it back to the shop and he's gone. The new manager has no idea what the other guy promised you, so the cycle starts over again.

Then you complain to the factory. The factory representative makes a deal with the service manager about how your car will be fixed. Before you have a chance to reap the rewards of this arrangement, the new service manager quits too, and you're back where you started. Meantime, the only decent mechanic in the place packed his tools and moved on to greener pastures at some other dealership. Sound impossible? I've seen this sort of thing happen over and over again.

To keep yourself out of this kind of mess, you simply must know how to evaluate a dealership service department and be able to recognize the obvious danger signals such as bad working conditions, unkempt mechanics, and even insufficient service equipment. To properly troubleshoot engine performance in modern cars, an *engine analyzer* (an automotive oscilloscope/exhaust gas analyzer) is a must. Other pieces of equipment the shop should have include a drive-on *wheel-alignment machine*, dynamic *wheel-balancing machine*, and a disc/drum *brake lathe*.

Ask the service manager to show you these important tools. Good shops are proud of their high-tech equipment and will be happy to have the chance to prove to you that they have it. Those that don't have it will likely cause you a lot of inconvenience. I've seen too many customers with steering and handling complaints unnecessarily lose the use of their cars for a full day because their dealers had to rely on independent wheel-alignment shops. In other cases, dealers have completely avoided taking any action on steering complaints because of not having wheel-alignment equipment.

The Service Manager

While you're checking out a service department, make sure you get a chance to talk to the service manager. Find out how long he's worked at the dealership you're considering. If he's new there, how long was the last guy there, and the one before him? If the place is a revolving-door operation for employees, the customers will get the revolving-door treatment too.

Just a word of caution about your first exposure to the service manager. Any good dealer will have no objection to introducing you to key people in the service department before you buy a new car. Just don't come across like you're putting them under a microscope. Tell the salesman you want to meet the service manager because you want to get acquainted with the person to whom you'll be entrusting a very valuable investment—your new car. Make sure you are introduced to the service manager, not just the service writers who are his subordinates. Usually, the service writers are not much more than service salesmen and have very little authority in the shop. If you can't reach the top man before you buy your new car, you'll likely find him even more heavily insulated from you after you sign on the dotted line. So, when you need help from him, you won't get it.

The Mechanics

When you meet the service manager, tell him you're interested in his policy regarding specialization in his shop. For example, if you need service because of some malfunction in the vehicle's computer-control system, can you expect that a technician specifically trained on that system will work on your car? Ask him about the credentials of his mechanics—have they attended manufacturer's training courses? Do they have certificates to demonstrate completion of the training programs? Ask to see them and check them carefully!

Minimally, you should see certificates covering air conditioning systems, automatic transmissions, engine tune-up and electrical systems, computer-control systems, antilock brake systems, power steering, rear-axle assemblies, charging systems, and engine overhaul. If you don't see credentials demonstrating competence in the model you are considering, ask the service manager for an explanation. He may tell you that there has not been a significant mechanical change since the certificate was issued, which could be true. Moreover, once a mechanic has been thoroughly trained in a particular system for a certain model, he can often learn a newer version by studying the manufacturer's technical literature instead of going to school again. However, if the shop's mechanics have not been to the factory school for a few years, look for another dealership, especially if you see no evidence of recent computer-systems training.

Regarding mechanic certification, you should know that there is a big difference between what is known as ASE certification and factory certification. ASE stands for Automotive Service Excellence. The credential is issued by the National Institute for Automotive Service Excellence to mechanics who pass certain written tests. The tests are broken down into categories covering brakes, transmissions, tune-up, and electrical work, etc. A mechanic who passes one of these written tests demonstrates general understanding of the topic, but not necessarily an understanding about your particular car. The reason is that the tests do not focus exclusively on individual vehicle makes such as Mercedes, Ford, etc. So what do ASE credentials tell you about mechanics who have them?

Most mechanics downplay the importance of ASE certification. They claim that the credentials only prove some guys know how to pass tests; not that they know how to fix cars. That's just a lot of sour grapes! The people who strongly criticize ASE certification are usually the most incompetent butchers in the industry. Even if all the tests do is prove that the participants know how to pass tests, at least they verify that the mechanics who take them can read. That's more than can be said for some of those out there who delude themselves into thinking they are automotive "technicians." Any mechanic who wants to keep up with the increasing complexity of today's cars better know how to read with good comprehension or he won't be able to understand automotive technical literature, which gets more complex every year.

Quite honestly, ASE certification *by itself* doesn't always mean a whole lot. A case in point was a mechanic who worked for me while I was a service manager at a Ford dealership. This guy had every ASE (in those days it was called NIASE) certification available. And yet, he had to be about the most useless fellow on Ford products I had ever run into. But he was exceptionally bright, really wanted to learn, and, yes, he was good at taking tests. So I invested a lot of the service department's money sending him to Ford technical schools for product-specific training. The results were amazing. After a while the guy became a wizard on Ford products and never ceased to astonish me with his diagnostic skill and repair capabilities. I never got the same results from mechanics who hadn't passed the ASE certification tests. The bottom line is that, at the very least, ASE certification indicates that a mechanic has the capacity to learn. The mechanic holding the certificate also demonstrates some professional pride. He can be counted on to be willing to improve his skills.

ASE critics argue that this form of voluntary certification is just a gimmick promoted by the automobile industry to forestall mandatory state licensing. That's a lot of bunk. ASE tests are pretty thorough, and it's doubtful that any the states could dream up would be more comprehensive. Besides, when was the last time you saw a state government administrate any program efficiently?

In the end, the taxpayer always foots the bill and you'll pay for both the licensing program and the increased auto-repair labor rates that will likely follow.

What about factory certification as an alternative to mechanic licensing? Is the so-called factory-trained technician really competent? Just how much does Mr. Goodwrench learn in General Motors' service schools? In short, plenty! Unfortunately, dealers don't always send their mechanics to factory schools. Under the terms of a dealer's franchise agreement with the manufacturer, mechanics must take factory-training courses. For reasons you'll discover later in this book, the franchise agreement is not always enforced. The consumer gets the short end of that deal.

Nevertheless, there are countless cynics out there making their reputations as consumer advocates who debunk the quality of auto manufacturers' training programs. These people speak from ignorance. Typically, they were never mechanics, they never managed a repair shop, and they never worked for an auto manufacturer. Yet they arrogantly presume to have keen insight into the problems besetting the auto industry. You might expect a plumber to give you as competent a judgment about your gallbladder trouble as these people can give you about the auto industry's problems.

Mr. Goodwrench learns plenty at General Motors' schools, as do mechanics who attend training programs run by any major auto manufacturer. The problem isn't the quality of the training; it's getting mechanics to attend the schools. That's where the dealers fall short. Too many automobile dealerships are owned by Stone-Age troglodytes who would rather spend money on colorful flags for their used-car lots than training their mechanics. Dealers of this ilk go bonkers at the thought of losing four hundred bucks in labor sales on a mechanic who spends a day in school. They just can't understand that training is an investment that pays off handsomely in the long run. So they play every conceivable game to avoid sending mechanics to factory schools, regardless of how much their customers suffer.

As an example, I remember a particular dealer I had the displeasure of having in my zone when I was a regional service manager with Volvo of America Corporation. The fellow who owned the place was a real sweetheart.

I heard rumors that he had sued his own father to get control of the operation—maybe that explained his less than exemplary concern for his customers. In fact, it seemed as though every car his shop touched turned into a colossal customer-relations nightmare, mostly because of technical incompetence.

After I leaned on the owner of the dealership to agree to send a mechanic to our factory school for much-needed training, a body ultimately appeared in one of our classrooms. I say a "body" because I think this student's motor activity was regulated by nerve impulses from his spinal cord instead of conscious thoughts from his brain. The guy was a real zombie! It seems he might have been recruited from a local gin mill for the assignment. Maybe his expertise was in gasohol. Anyway, the ruse didn't work and the dealer was put on formal notice that he was in violation of his franchise agreement.

This was the kind of dealer every auto manufacturer dreads. Concerned only with sales, his service department was the farthest thing from his mind. Dealers of this ilk can be depended on to stubbornly ignore any of the manufacturer's efforts to upgrade their mechanics' technical skills. Sending nonessential, unqualified people to training classes is a common ploy. Some dealers don't even bother playing that game, preferring outright refusal when it comes to answering the factory's demand for mechanic training. I witnessed a case like this firsthand when I was a service director at a Nissan dealership.

The dealer was a drunk who used to drive the factory people to despair with his insane antics and refusal to cooperate on any matters of potential benefit to his customers, including training. Apparently, the factory representative had given him some flak about his delinquency in this area. The dealer's response showed just what a delinquent he was. I guess he was trying to make some kind of a statement by not driving a Datsun anymore. So he began showing up at about 11:00 A.M. almost every day in his used ("previously owned") Mercedes. Now, mind you, this character did not have a Mercedes franchise. Compared to the little Datsuns we were selling, the Mercedes was so huge that the people in the shop fondly referred to it as a parade float.

Predictably, this barge on wheels could be heard in the morning outside the shop doors, horn blasting, its half-sober driver anxious to get into the service area. Once inside, our beloved dealer would wobble over to my office and pound on my desk, raving about the urgency of stopping all work in the shop to service his beloved parade float. The pathetic rum-soaked wretch couldn't care less that his customers would not have their cars' warranty work done because he was interrupting the normal work flow in the service department. With the threat of firing everybody in the shop he always got his way. The customers suffered. But, oh, did his Mercedes purr!

One morning things finally got out of hand. As usual, the parade float came screeching through the shop doors. Only this time a real live parade followed it! My wacky boss had some buddies in the circus business who needed work on their vehicles, so he had their whole damn caravan follow him into the shop. In absolute shock I dropped my buttered bagel and a cup of hot coffee on myself when I saw a tractor-trailer pull in, the rear doors open, and some bozo dressed in a clown's costume fly out of the trailer on a motorcycle.

That was the last straw. The hell with the customers—I

made haste to the drugstore for some ointment for my burns and went home to clean up my résumé. I think Nissan Motors later had the good sense to terminate the dealer's franchise, shortly after which cirrhosis of the liver terminated the dealer. But what hell the poor customers went through trying to get warranty work while all that was going on!

However, had they surveyed the shop and asked the right questions before buying a car there, they could have avoided the grief. In the two years prior to my employment, the service department had seen six service managers come and go. Mechanics regularly quit because of deplorable working conditions. Naturally, the lush who owned the dealership wouldn't pay to send the replacements to school, so there were, of course, no training certificates displayed anywhere in the building. It would have been worth it for customers intent on buying a Datsun (an excellent car by the way) to have traveled fifteen miles to a nearby dealership operated by a reputable businessman who hadn't had his brain chemically lobotomized by alcohol.

I've told this story and the one about the Volvo dealer to a few acquaintances who have asked me whether it implies something negative about foreign car manufacturers, at least as far as their commitment to mechanic training. The answer is no. Car companies don't go out of their way to give franchises to dealers who won't take competent service seriously. A dealer can appear to have the best of intentions initially, only to gravitate into ineptitude later on. The point to keep in mind is that even fine companies like Volvo and Nissan can get stuck with lousy dealers. Every other manufacturer, foreign and domestic, has the same problem. So, never assume that a prestige car line and great service go hand in hand.

In fact, that's a mistake a lot of consumers make when they buy an imported car. The foreign manufacturers have done a good job brainwashing the American motoring public into believing that mechanics who work on foreign cars are better trained than those who work on domestic makes. I guess people believe what they need to, to justify spending so much money on mystique. I've seen no evidence that indicates to me that Mercedes-Benz or BMW have better training programs for their dealer mechanics than Ford, Chrysler, or General Motors. I have noticed, though, that anybody named Horst or Hans who's carrying a wrench in his right hand is assumed to have some mystical mechanical powers.

This calls to mind a Mercedes dealership I worked for. Their resident technical guru was an affable, yet somewhat arrogant, character named Heinrich (we affectionately called him Field Marshal Heinrich). Most of the customers thought he was from Bavaria. In fact, I think he was from the Lower East Side of New York City, where he spent a lot of time employed as a plumber. But Heinrich enjoyed the myth too much to pop anybody's bubble. The customers just adored his German accent, and had the highest reverence for his white lab coat— you'd think the guy was a brain surgeon!

Anyway, in terms of service department revenue, Heinrich was worth his weight in gold, because the customers believed anything he told them, even though he often seemed to confuse carburetors and gas tanks with toilet bowls and cesspools. No matter that Heinrich couldn't always get the terminology straight. The other people in the shop who did know what they were talking about usually bailed him out when things got sticky.

So much for the myth of the European-trained auto technician. You'll find charlatans like Heinrich in Porsche shops, BMW shops, Audi and Volkswagen shops, and even in Alfa Romeo, Ferrari, and Maserati shops. They're usually no more competent than the people working in Chevy service departments, but they're generally more arrogant, and often not smart enough to know just how much they don't know.

I remember this guy Guido who was the head mechanic in a dealership I routinely visited while I was a regional service manager with Alfa Romeo, Inc., the U.S. distributor of the Italian-made sports cars. It was only after much cajoling that I was able to convince Guido that I should be given the opportunity to show him how to use an exhaust gas analyzer to check the fuel mixture on an Alfa Romeo. Guido insisted he didn't need any fancy newfangled test equipment to find out how well a car was running. As he put it: "I'm-a listen-a, I'm-a touch-a, then I fix-a." So confident was Guido in his auditory and tactile senses that he thought he only had to listen to an Alfa engine and touch it with his hands to be able to completely diagnose malfunctions in its fuel-injection system. A few minutes into his first tutorial on the exhaust gas analyzer and Guido himself saw that he was full of pasta.

So, when you're considering a certain dealership as the source of your new car, don't be misled by the service mystique normally associated with imported models. And don't be too impressed by white lab coats in the shop. Also, don't select a dealership solely on the basis of lowest price offered! Be objective and look for average or above-average CSI ratings, service excellence awards, training certificates, and other hard evidence of a quality service department. In most cases, you would be better off paying a few hundred dollars more to buy your car from a dealership with a good service department.

4

▼ ▼ ▼

Making Sure Your Car Gets Fixed Under Warranty

If you have purchased your new car from a reputable dealership with a good service department, getting your car fixed under warranty shouldn't be too difficult. If your dealer has an incompetent service department, you could be in big trouble. Unfortunately, there are many inept automobile dealers who simply have no interest in doing warranty work. Considering how often consumers fail to get problems with their new cars corrected, this should come as no big revelation. What may surprise you is that there are aspects of the automobile service industry that sometimes discourage even excellent dealers from wanting to fix your car under warranty.

How the Warranty System Works

Not long ago, the reasons for this were far more obvious than they are now. Typically, manufacturers paid much lower hourly labor rates for warranty work than dealers charged for customer-paid repairs. A shop billing $25 per hour for customer-paid labor might have received only $15 per hour from the factory for warranty jobs. This began to change in the 1970s when some states passed legislation requiring that auto manufacturers pay warranty labor rates on a par with their dealers' customer labor rates. The assumption was that the unequal labor rate structure was at the root of many customers' complaints about the inability to get their cars fixed under warranty. Eventually, many car manufacturers voluntarily made labor rate parity a rule of thumb in every state.

With dealers everywhere getting the same hourly compensation for factory-paid warranty work as customer-paid labor, you might expect that no dealers would be reluctant to take care of warranty complaints. Yet many are, and for what they consider very good reasons. Even if the factory pays the same hourly rate for labor (which it actually does not, in spite of apparent warranty labor parity), it doesn't pay the dealer as much for parts. For a warranty repair, the dealer is limited to an arbitrary gross profit on any replaced parts. The margin allowed by the factory could be 20 or 30 percent, or whatever formula it wants to use. So, as an example, let's say your car is under warranty and it needs a new brake caliper. If the dealership's parts department must pay the factory $100 to buy a caliper, the dealer might be reimbursed $130 for the part when it is used to repair your car—a 30 percent gross profit.

Why Dealers Don't Want to Do Warranty Work

Sounds pretty clean and simple, right? Well, not quite, because the transaction gets complicated along the way. For the dealer to get paid, an employee must fill out a warranty claim form. A record of the claim must be made in a ledger. The malfunctioning brake caliper must be tagged and retained by the parts department until such time as a factory representative inspects it and certifies it defective. In some cases, the factory may want the dealer to return the part with the corresponding warranty claim. All this takes time. And it costs the dealer money. It will cost him a lot more if the factory rejects the warranty claim, insisting that the brake caliper is not really defective. In this case, the service manager and the parts manager could get into a argument with the factory representative over the disputed part—more lost time, more lost money.

Now, consider how easy it is for the dealer to avoid this hassle. The service manager just gives you some line of bull in response to your brake complaint for as long as it takes for your warranty to expire. At that point, one of his mechanics finds a problem with a caliper and replaces it. Naturally, you pay. But unlike the factory, you don't get hit with a 20 or 30 percent markup. The caliper the dealer paid $100 for is billed to you at $200—a 100 percent gross profit. After you pay the bill, the dealer takes your money to the bank, and your old caliper is heaved into the trash can.

You'll notice that I haven't said anything yet about the labor bill. So far you might have assumed that with factories paying the same labor rates as you do, there should be no difference in the amount billed for a mechanic's time. In fact, there is a big enough difference to dampen a dealer's enthusiasm for doing warranty work. For most parts replacement tasks, the factory fixes the amount of time it will pay under warranty. The manufacturer provides its dealers with a labor time guidebook containing a coded list of repairs and the allocated time for each repair. For your brake caliper, the person preparing the warranty claim looks up the code for a caliper replacement on your car model and the allocated time. The code and the time are recorded on the warranty claim. If the factory guidebook allows only one hour for replacement of a caliper, that's all the dealer will be paid for labor on that job. So, if the labor rate is $50 per hour, the factory pays the dealer exactly $50, not a penny more.

Now let's see what happens when you're paying the bill. Instead of using the factory labor time guidebook, the dealer may use an independent time guide called a flat-rate manual. These manuals are published by various large automotive publishing firms, which cater very heavily to the aftermarket. Put simply, the aftermarket is that part of the auto industry not including the factories and their authorized dealers. Your independent neighborhood garage then is part of the aftermarket. Typically, the aftermarket doesn't get the cream of the crop when it comes to service work. The cars that the independent shops handle are usually older, dirtier, and harder to work on. Consequently, the times allowed in the flat-rate manuals are more liberal than those posted in the factory warranty labor time guides. So the brake caliper replacement that gets an allowance of one hour in the factory guide may have one and a half hours allocated in the flat-rate manual. At $50 per hour, you'll get a bill for $75, instead of the $50 in labor paid by the factory for the same repair.

Some dealers look at these economics and decide that warranty work is just not their cup of tea. What happens to you if you buy your new car from a dealer with this attitude? Obviously, not much when you come back looking for warranty service—you simply may not get any service. Of course, after your warranty expires, the same dealer could convey a whole new attitude about fixing your car. Unfortunately, the change of heart may not be accompanied by the competence to get the job done. The reason for this is that the dealers who have the strongest aversion to doing warranty work are usually the most technically inept. And they sure don't get any better at fixing cars when you're paying the bill instead of the factory.

Even though the factory may pay less for warranty repairs than a dealer gets for customer-paid work, efficient dealers can still do warranty work profitably. The issue isn't really that you may be willing to pay $75 for a repair for which the factory only allows $50. What the dealer has to worry about is whether he can make a profit at $50. If his shop can do the job on your car at that price and make some money on it, there's no reason for him to want to avoid doing warranty work on your car.

Having managed a few dealership service departments (including Ford, Chrysler, and Nissan), I'm convinced that warranty work can be profitable if the shop is properly supervised and the mechanics are competent. Normally, the factory will not pay for the same repair twice. Contrast that with many unsuspecting customers who get bled over and over again for slipshod repairs attributable to incorrect diagnoses. Manufacturers have little tolerance for this nonsense. They expect their dealers to diagnose a problem quickly and to fix it right the first time. That takes exceptional knowledge of the automobile being worked on, a lot of mechanical skill, and all the appropriate test equipment.

Good supervision, good mechanics, and good tools all cost money—a lot more than many dealers are willing to spend. The average new car dealership is owned by a person whose background is in car sales, not service. Typically, these people are not service-oriented. In fact, they often view service as an annoying, losing proposition because they have little or no knowledge of what it takes to operate a service department profitably. All they want to do is sell cars, and let the factory worry about fixing them.

You'll find this attitude quite frequently in the major metropolitan markets. With the available customer pool running into the millions, dealers in these markets often don't care that good service may inspire customer loyalty and repeat sales.As a case in point, I remember a Long Island dealership that was in my zone when I was a regional service manager with Alfa Romeo. The guy who owned the place was a super salesman who, with clever advertising, was able to draw customers from all over the New York metropolitan area and even as far as New Jersey and Pennsylvania. He sold other car lines besides Alfa Romeo, and his shop was far too small to handle the service volume. The result? Many of his customers did not get warranty service. Consequently, Alfa Romeo's customer-relations office was deluged with complaints about the dealership. It was my job to solve this problem.

Using the standard company line in a personal meeting with the dealer, I pointed out to him that he was establishing a bad reputation and could not expect repeat purchases or good referrals from customers who had gotten a raw deal in his service department. He had to enlarge the shop, hire better mechanics, and spend money to get them trained. He also had to buy much needed diagnostic equipment. At that, he proceeded to lecture me on his philosophy of selling cars in a big city. "Who do you think drives Rolls-Royces and lives in mansions in this town?" he asked me. "I'll tell you," he continued, without even permitting a reply. "It's not the 'nice guy' car dealers who spend a fortune on good service departments to take care of their customers. It's not the 'nice guys' who waste their time doing warranty work for peanuts. It's the ruthless bastards like me who use their smarts to sell the most cars and rape every dumb shithead who walks into the showroom. Who cares about repeat sales to these jerks? I want maximum bucks per sale, that's all. I screw a thousand morons out there and there are millions more of them in this city ready to come and buy a car from me because they believe my advertising and my sales rap."

After much cajoling I won some concessions from him, only because he respected me personally. There was no way to convince him that doing warranty work competently would be in his best interest. And neither Alfa Romeo nor any other factory from which he got a franchise had the horsepower to muscle this guy into compliance with good service practices. He ultimately acceded to my pleas that he do something about his griping customers because he felt bad that they were making my job unbearable for me. Not wishing to torment me further with additional customer-relations headaches, he ordered his service manager to give priority treatment to Alfa's warranty-related complaints.

Dealers like him can be found everywhere, not just in big cities. An aversion to matters pertaining to service and warranty work is often second nature to dealership owners who came up the ranks through the sales department. When you buy a car from one of these people, you may not stand a good chance of getting fair treatment when warranty work is needed. This is the kind of dealer who blames the factory for all the problems you may have with your car, with the often-used cop-out, "we don't build 'em, we only fix 'em." And then of course they proceed not to "fix 'em," because they don't want to do warranty work "for peanuts" as the Alfa dealer on Long Island put it.

How Good Dealers Beat the Warranty System to the Benefit of Their Customers

Even though there is more money in customer-paid labor than in warranty work, smart dealers are clever enough to make up for the shortfall for their own and their customers' benefit. They just do a little creative gouging when it comes to billing the factory for warranty repairs. And if the manufacturer's customer relations department isn't getting a ton of complaints from such a dealer, padded warranty claims will probably be ignored. So that you can see just how much a shrewd dealer is capable of doing to help a customer under warranty, I'll tell you a little about how the warranty system works.

Automobile manufacturers maintain expense statistics that show the average cost per unit (CPU) under warranty. To see what CPU really means, let's suppose the 1990 DreamMobile you bought is one of 100,000 total vehicles of that model sold by the manufacturer in that model year. Let's assume that nationwide $10,000,000 worth of warranty work is done on 1990 DreamMobiles. The warranty cost per unit is $10,000,000 divided by 100,000, or $100 per car. Now remember, that's an average CPU. Some cars can have a lot more than $100 worth of warranty work performed on them. Others can have a lot less.

The manufacturers' warranty statistics don't stop at CPU. They also have figures showing costs by region, such as northeast United States, southeast, etc. The numbers are further broken down to costs by service zone or district. New York City is one district, for example, southern Connecticut another, and so on. And then the figures are broken down to cost by individual dealership. Suppose, for example, that you bought your DreamMobile from ABC Motors, a dealership that sold 100 of them, while billing the factory $20,000 in warranty work. Divide $20,000 by 100 cars and you'll see that ABC Motors has a warranty CPU of $200, double the national average. Just why is ABC Motors billing twice as much warranty work as the average dealership? There are lots of possible explanations. They could be submitting phony warranty claims to make up for all the work the factory doesn't pay for. Or, they could be padding the claims to make up the difference between what the factory pays and what a customer would pay for nonwarranty work. Or, they could be just crooks.

The factory can take a variety of actions including sending in a team of auditors if it suspects warranty fraud, the submission of falsified claims. As a practical matter, the factory will probably do nothing if the dealer is selling lots of cars and his customers are happy. If the manufacturer is not receiving many complaints about the dealer's service, he can assume that the customers are satisfied.

Knowing that the factory reasons this way, good dealers will exploit the system to assist their customers. In some cases, even if your car is beyond warranty, your dealer may be able to fix it free without losing money. Suppose your car's warranty expired 3,000 miles ago and now it has a bad wheel bearing. You feel the part was failing while the warranty was in effect. The service manager sympathizes with you because you're a good customer—you always have your car serviced in his shop. To help you out, he has a mechanic replace your car's wheel bearing and then he processes a warranty claim against another customer's car whose warranty has not yet expired. Don't underestimate the importance of the gesture. He could get caught, because many parts are stamped with special codes that facilitate tracing them to a particular vehicle identification number. Also, he has to process a lot of extra paper work to cover his tracks. But he'll go out on the limb for you because you're a valued customer.

Because of recent developments in consumer law, dealers are almost forced to file some falsified warranty claims to assist their customers. A few years ago, a service manager who had a good working rapport with the factory could easily get a warranty extension for a car owner in need of special help. These warranty extensions were described by a variety of terms, including "goodwill" adjustments, "policy" adjustments, and other names depending on the manufacturer. Some of these so-called adjustments were interpreted by the Federal Trade Commission as secret warranties, which should have been available to every customer under similar circumstances. After numerous lawsuits and millions of dollars in legal fees and settlements, manufacturers became somewhat less liberal about the dispensation of "goodwill" adjustments applied to vehicles whose warranty had expired.

But there's still plenty of flexibility where unexpired warranties are concerned. I've seen dealers come up with all sorts of bizarre scams to generate bogus warranty claims, often to cover legitimate work on cars with expired warranties. Occasionally, manufacturers send out questionnaires to people on whose cars warranty work was reported for the purpose of verifying that the work was actually done. These surveys help the factory catch the crooked dealers out there who randomly submit claims on cars that were never in their shops. Factory representatives can also check service department appointment schedules and other records to confirm that a particular vehicle was in the shop on the date a warranty repair was claimed. Knowing this, some dealers go to great efforts to ensure that a constant flow of warranty-eligible vehicles pass through their shops so that plenty of bogus claims can be generated.

One of the more creative techniques I've seen involves sending a mailgram to every customer whose warranty is about to expire. The mailgram notifies the owner of the impending expiration of the warranty and emphasizes the need for a free inspection of the entire car. The dealer offers to check out the car and fix any defects free of charge before the warranty lapses. In some cases the car is actually repaired. In others, the customer is told that a certain repair was done, even though it wasn't. If surveyed by the factory, that customer believes his car was fixed and expresses his satisfaction with the courteous treatment he got from the dealer. The money collected from the factory for the fictitious repair pays for a legitimate repair on some other customer's car. Or maybe, it just goes into the till to help subsidize heavy discounting of the selling price of new cars. For example, if the dealer can squeeze $50 in fake warranty work out of every car he sells, he can afford to drop the selling price by $50 and be that much more competitive than other dealers in his area.

Either way, the customer benefits by buying a car from a dealership like this. If the dealer is smart enough to get away with his warranty scam, he can afford to sell cars cheaper than the competition. And later, he can afford to fix cars free that other dealers would charge their customers for, making them satisfied, potentially repeat buyers. Pretty good business sense isn't it?

Get a Pre-Expiration Warranty Inspection

Don't let another important lesson here pass you by. Regardless of whether or not your dealer sends you a mailgram soliciting a last-minute warranty inspection, get one done anyway. Even if you have to pay an independent mechanic to thoroughly go over your car from bumper to bumper just before your warranty expires, it will probably be worth it. Have him look for things like incipient oil leaks from engine and transmission seals. Ask him to check for oil stains around air conditioning fittings that could be indicative of the need for new "O" rings, tubing repairs, and additional refrigerant. Make sure he inspects the power-steering pump for leaks, and the steering rack for fluid leaks. There are dozens of other areas he can examine besides these. Get a written report of his findings and take a copy to your dealer and request immediate warranty attention. Later in this chapter I'll tell you how to present your requests so that you maximize your chances to get what you are entitled to under warranty.

By getting a thorough inspection just before your warranty expires you can maximize the value of your car's warranty. Many consumers purchase extended warranties, which in some cases are good investments. Nevertheless, the same consumers who spend a great deal of money on an extended warranty fail to exploit the basic warranty for all that it is worth.

For example, let's suppose your car has a 36,000-mile warranty. A mechanic inspects the vehicle at 35,500 miles and finds that both front struts have leaked significantly, requiring installation of new strut cartridges. By bringing this problem to the attention of the selling dealership you can have the work done under warranty free of charge. Assuming the struts last at least 35,500 additional miles, you will benefit from the use of the new parts for that period of time. You will have maximized the value of your warranty and minimized your long-term maintenance costs. In this example, the $50 inspection will have saved you as much as $300 in repairs. A reputable car dealer will have no objection to accommodating your request for warranty work in a situation like this.

As you can see, a dealer can indeed make an enormous difference when it comes to getting good results with your car's warranty problems. This is just as true with vehicles that are well within warranty as those whose warranties have recently expired. Most consumers mistakenly believe that auto manufacturers treat all their dealers equally. Based on this assumption, they conclude that all dealers have equal authority to make required warranty repairs. Nothing could be farther from the truth.

Why Auto Manufacturers Treat Some Car Dealers Better Than Others, and How That Affects You

In a utopian society manufacturers would in fact treat all their dealers impartially. In the real world it doesn't work that way. The manufacturer or "factory" is not some totally impartial and unbiased abstract entity. It's a bunch of people with typical human prejudices and tendencies toward favoritism. Consequently, as a consumer, you would be denying human nature if you thought one dealership is as good as another in terms of its power to assist you under warranty. The factory has favorites when it comes to its franchised dealers. The "good guys" go on the list of favorites. The "bad guys" wind up on the proverbial "shit list." It's important for you to buy from one of the "good guys" because they can give their customers a lot more than the outcasts. Why? Simply because they have the latitude to interpret the warranty more flexibly.

Just how does a dealer become either a factory favorite or an outcast, and how does that affect you in a practical way? First, you have to understand that auto companies have split personalities. One side cares only about sales. These are the guys in the sales and marketing division. If a dealer is selling a lot of cars, he's a hero, at least to the sales division. The other side of an auto company's personality is service oriented—the service division. These people get all the flak when cars aren't being fixed properly by the dealers. If a dealer sells a lot of cars but also creates a lot of service complaints, he's a bum as far as the service division is concerned.

Factory service people are quite human and can get fed up with hostile consumers who take their problems with dealers' service departments out on them. You can only handle so many complaints before you burn out. And burnout is fairly common among factory service management personnel whose job it is to regularly visit franchised dealerships to help solve customers' service problems. Most of these problems are created by dealership incompetence, so it's understandable that the factory representative might grow to resent a dealership that frequently dumps its disgruntled customers in his lap. When the factory representative gets disgusted with a dealership, he's less inclined to cooperate with the service department and less likely to respond favorably to its requests on behalf of its customers.

For example, if he does his job by the book, he might be required by his company to personally inspect any car that needs repainting or upholstery work under warranty. If he gets along well with a service manager and trusts that manager's judgment, he could empower him to proceed with paint or upholstery work on his own initiative. How would that benefit you as a consumer? Well, for one thing, you would not have to leave your car at the dealership for a whole day just to have some guy from the factory look at it. Furthermore, if the factory representative did see it, he could potentially discover that your paint problem was due to industrial fallout, or some other kind of chemical damage not covered by warranty. Or he could determine that your upholstery damage was caused by your child having raked a toy screwdriver across the back seat. If your dealer's service manager does his job well and doesn't give the factory a lot of grief, the factory will give him what he wants and you'll get your car fixed free of charge and free of hassles. Remember, factory people are just that—people, with normal human inclinations. So, as far as they are concerned, one hand washes the other. If the service manager is a klutz and the entire service department is a chronic headache to the factory, his requests for special consideration relevant to paint and upholstery might meet with a very rigid interpretation of the warranty, that is, claim denied! Sure, the innocent customer could wind up paying for the dealer's sins. But isn't that the way things work every day in the real world anyway, where human nature often wins out over logic?

I vividly remember an example of human nature at work both to the detriment and later the benefit of the customers at a certain Ford dealership where I was the service manager. Having previously spent so much time in the imported-car business, I had let myself get a bit brainwashed by the industry scuttlebutt about domestic auto manufacturers not taking as good care of their customers as foreign-car companies. If Ford was an indication, that couldn't have been farther from the truth. In fact, I can honestly say, I have never seen a company do more for its customers or offer more service assistance to its dealers than Ford.

When I took the job at this dealership, the service department had been losing money every month for years. Customer complaints were running rampant. None of the mechanics had any recent Ford service schooling. Previous service managers refused to cooperate with any suggestions Ford offered to improve the service department. The situation was so bad that the factory district service manager and customer relations manager had apparently begun to grow deaf to complaints originating at this dealership—not surprising considering that all their best efforts were regularly thwarted by the bungling jerks who worked there.

My deal with the owner of the dealership was that I would be given a free hand to implement whatever corrections I deemed necessary to solve the shop's problems if I could make the service department profitable. To the owner's amazement, I turned a handsome profit the very first month. Immediately, I began sending mechanics to school almost weekly. I assured Ford that I would do everything possible to satisfy any Ford owner who had been ripped off by this dealership if Ford would cooperate with me and meet me half way. Ford absolutely shocked me. Everybody on their staff in the zone office went an extra mile to provide both technical assistance and money under a liberal interpretation of the warranty. Virtually anything I asked for on behalf of a Ford customer was granted. In return, I personally saw to it that every car with a problem was fixed properly and that its owner left the service department happy.

The experience demonstrated to me that Ford had some first-class people in their service organization. All they wanted from a dealership was a sincere effort at taking care of Ford owners. Upon getting this, it seemed as though their generosity was almost limitless. Human nature is such that most people will reward sincere effort on their behalf and reciprocate with gratitude and cooperation. The people at Ford showed me they had a human side to them that went way beyond what was required of them "by the book."

What was really interesting about the Ford dealership I worked at was how customers who swore they would never buy another Ford, later walked into the showroom looking for another Ford as a second car. Obviously, it was previously lousy service that turned these people off to Fords, not any intrinsic inferiority in the product. So why, you may wonder, didn't Ford shut this dealership down earlier if they cared so much about the plight of their customers? Well, for the same reason other manufacturers don't terminate the franchises of schlock dealers under similar circumstances. This dealership sold a pretty fair number of new cars, and under our legal system, when a dealer is selling well, it's almost impossible for the factory to cancel the dealer's franchise. The litigation costs are beyond belief, and the manufacturer usually loses in court. Does that surprise you? Since when in

America does the bad guy always get the lumps in court he deserves? That being the case, manufacturers are forced to do business with a lot of rotten car dealers until such time as they wither on the vine and blow away— something they eventually all do.

However, in the process they make a lot of customers miserable, either by deliberately evading their responsibilities to perform warranty work, or failing to adequately represent their customers' best interests in their dealings with the factory. Unfortunately, to make sure his customers always get a fair shake under warranty, a service manager has to go beyond being a nice guy and running an efficient shop. The big auto manufacturers in many respects behave like government bureaucracies, burdened with rules and regulations that sometimes make little sense and must be broken to get anything done. Knowing how to "beat the system" is an important skill for a service manager to have if he is going to successfully work with any automobile company bureaucracy. His skill, or lack of it, will have a major impact on how you are treated under warranty.

A good example of this involves the increasing application of sophisticated electronics to automobiles. While it's true that electronics technology has done a lot to improve automobile performance, there is a downside for car owners. Consumers will likely experience problems getting their cars repaired because the auto manufacturers make it tough for their dealers to process warranty claims against malfunctioning electronic parts. The auto companies generally require that their dealers return all major electronic components replaced under warranty. These parts are then tested to make sure they are really defective. That is where the trouble starts.

Let's say you bring your new car into ABC Motors because it sometimes won't start, particularly in very cold weather. A mechanic checks it out with special test equipment and can't identify a malfunction. Yet, based on his experience, he decides it needs a new ignition module, an electronic part that is partially responsible for generating a spark at the spark plugs. The module is replaced and it is sent back to the factory along with a warranty claim. Subsequently, the factory tests the module and finds it is functioning normally. They reject the warranty claim, refusing to pay the dealer, and then send the part back. Meanwhile, the new module has completely solved the starting trouble you had with your car.

Some dealers can be intimidated by rejected claims such as this one, and decide that they won't replace any ignition modules anymore under warranty unless their test equipment can clearly define a defect. When your car is examined by such a dealer, you become a victim of the bureaucracy, because they'll send you away claiming they couldn't find a problem with your car. The next time it gets cold out, your vehicle will wind up on a tow hook.

Tricks Good Service Managers Use to Help Their Customers

A dealership with a competent service manager won't let you be victimized by bureaucratic red tape. Instead of arguing with the factory over whether or not your ignition module is really defective, he'll order one of his mechanics to replace it with a new part. Later, the mechanic will connect the terminals of the original module to a source of very high voltage, destroying its sensitive electronic components. This time when the factory tests it, the service manager can be damned sure they'll find it defective.

Good service departments sabotage suspect parts on behalf of their customers so that new ones can be installed in their cars under warranty without fear of rejected claims. On the other hand, second-rate service departments give their customers all kinds of lame excuses. "We can't find any problem—it seems to be working okay now." Or, "you'll have to leave it with us for a few days so we can see if the problem occurs." These jerks could spare their customers so much misery and inconvenience if they knew what they were doing and knew how to handle the factory bureaucracy.

Over the years I've personally witnessed dozens of intermittent problems caused by defective electrical or electronic components that were given a clean bill of health by test equipment. I'll never forget an incident involving Ben Jacobs, the owner of a Chrysler dealership (where I was head mechanic) and the district service manager from Chrysler's zone office. Jacobs was using a brand-new Chrysler, which he really loved. Unfortunately, when the cold winds of January blew in, his Chrysler preferred hibernation to cruising snow-covered highways—it just wouldn't start at temperatures below 15°F. Jacobs was a real believer in good service, so he invested in the latest and greatest test equipment. We put his car through every test conceivable and came up with nothing, so we replaced a few parts and hoped for the best.

Well, one day Chrysler's district service manager was visiting our dealership, so Jacobs offered to buy him lunch. The temperature outside was about 10°F, so wouldn't you know it—Jacobs's Chrysler didn't start. They took the district service manager's car instead, giving the shop another opportunity to get to the bottom of this bizarre problem. I suspected an intermittent open (an occasional incomplete circuit) in the ignition coil. Unfortunately, my suspicions were not confirmed by objective testing. Every check in the book said the coil was okay, and it put out perfectly normal secondary voltage when tested dynamically. While I was looking under the hood,

Jacobs and the factory man returned from lunch. I made the mistake of telling this eager beaver from Chrysler what was going on, at which time he cautioned me against replacing the ignition coil under warranty because he would look for the claim and see to it that it got rejected. "We don't pay for the replacement of perfectly good parts" he confidently asserted. Jacobs just shook his head and urged the district manager to join him in his office. Shortly thereafter, Jacobs came back out to the shop and ordered us to remove the coil from the district manager's car and replace it with the "perfectly good part" from his Chrysler. We were delighted to hear that the district service manager got stranded the very next day, courtesy of the supposedly good ignition coil.

As a service manager with a Ford dealership I saw many late 1970s and early 1980s models roll in at the end of a tow line when the weather got bitterly cold. In virtually every case the ignition amplifier was the culprit. And in every case the units tested out okay on test equipment supplied by Ford. We didn't want to hassle our customers, so we just gave them new amplifiers under warranty and deliberately burned out the old ones. As good as Ford was, they had rules to live by, so we just made it easier for them to play the game by their own rule book.

Why Some Cars Seem to Have the Same Defects Year After Year

Regardless of the best intentions on the part of a manufacturer's service personnel, they still have company politics to deal with when it comes to acknowledging that certain parts are indeed defective. Many consumers can't understand why an auto company would build cars having the same apparent defects year after year when changing a design would seem to be the logical solution. Even car dealers, who are often pretty savvy about such matters, get frustrated at the factory's reluctance to implement a design change that everybody knows is necessary. Even more frustrating to them is the fact that factory service people will often stick to the rule book when it comes to testing certain parts that dealers have replaced under warranty, for example, electronic parts that don't work in the car but function properly on a test bench.

Why do auto companies sometimes adhere to these illogical and impractical service policies? Simple, it's politics! Let's suppose a certain electronic widget has been failing over and over again in customers' cars. These widgets are tested by the manufacturer and check out, so the warranty claims are rejected and the parts are returned to the dealers. Are the factory service people so dumb and blind that they fanatically believe the widgets are good even though the dealers insist they don't work in a car? No, they're not that crazy. They're just trying to hold onto their jobs.

Quite possibly, the electronic widget causing all the problems was the brainchild of some high-level design engineer who got his company, DreamMobile Motors, to spend millions of dollars putting it into production. His design team came up with the widget's specifications, which were later given to the Acme Electronics Corporation. DreamMobile signed a contract with Acme to have them build 1,000,000 widgets to DreamMobile's specifications. Later, it's discovered that the widgets were not properly designed to function in the environment in which they are being installed under the DreamMobile's hood. DreamMobile blames Acme. Acme tells them to jump in a lake—the widgets were manufactured correctly to DreamMobile's specifications. So DreamMobile is on the hook for 1,000,000 widgets, many of which will probably fail in normal use.

Now, what does our brilliant design engineer do? Humbly admit his screw-up and recommend a new design? Offer to quit in an act of contrition? Shoot himself in the head? No, none of these. He'll stonewall the problem for as long as possible by just refusing to acknowledge that it exists. And eventually, all the DreamMobiles equipped with the temperamental widgets will go out of warranty. In the meantime, his staff will issue a directive to the people in the service division, ordering them to subject all incoming widgets returned under warranty to bench-testing. Does our shrewd design engineer know that the suggested bench tests might not identify the defect causing the widget to fail? Is he aware that many of them will be given a clean bill of health and returned to the dealers with their warranty claims rejected? Let's not underestimate this guy's self-preservation instincts.

And let's not underestimate the preparedness of the people in the service division to go along with this charade. Bucking a top-echelon engineering directive could be grounds for dismissal. So the official company line stands—widgets that test well on the bench are deemed satisfactory and do not qualify for reimbursement under the warranty. They are returned to the dealers with instructions that they be placed in parts inventory for installation in some other cars, where they might actually work, for a while anyway.

As I said before, good dealers know how to work around these absurd edicts coming from the factory bureaucracy. They'll just burn the widgets out completely. When the factory technicians test them according to the directive issued by the engineering honcho, the widgets will fail. So, they can confidently authorize payment of the warranty claims without rocking the engineer's boat and without fear of losing their jobs.

Computers in Cars: A Blessing or a Curse?

During my years working for auto manufacturers I've seen numerous cases where company politics stood in the way of sensible service solutions, especially where electronic components were involved. In every case though, dealers who were good at bending the rules were able to fix their customers' cars. This kind of flexibility is going to become more significant to consumers as computers assume greater importance in modern automobiles. Used in automotive applications, computers offer many advantages, among them better engine performance, improved fuel economy, reduced air pollution, and extension of maintenance intervals. On the downside, they introduce a level of complexity into automotive service that many people in the industry are incapable of dealing with. As a result, the signs are already pointing to big problems for new car owners in the near future.

Before solid-state electronics became commonplace in automotive systems, getting engine-performance problems fixed was no big deal. An engine that wouldn't run well might have been easily restored to healthy operation with a new carburetor, a new set of points and a condenser, or even a simple adjustment. Diagnosis was relatively easy, and repairs were inexpensive to implement. That's no longer true. A modern automobile is equipped with a fuel injection system instead of a simple carburetor. Fuel quantity and mixture are regulated by a computer, which receives various signals from sensors and transducers. These signals are interpreted by the computer, which in turn sends control commands to the fuel-injection system. The number of interactive parts is quite high in relation to comparatively primitive carburetor-equipped cars. So, identifying the source of a malfunction is proportionately more difficult. Compounding this is the fact that the computer is also handling other responsibilities besides controlling fuel mixture. For example, ignition timing may be under computer control, as well as various ignition characteristics during engine cranking and starting.

As a motorist you reap the benefits of better performance than could be achieved in noncomputerized automobiles—when your car runs. When it doesn't, you're in for a rough time getting it fixed, even if your car is under warranty. The auto industry spares no propaganda when it comes to touting the improved reliability and reduced maintenance costs attributable to computerization of modern automobiles. What the industry isn't so quick to admit is that fixing these computerized marvels is a far more difficult and expensive proposition than was the case with technologically less-sophisticated cars.

Auto mechanics have traditionally been least competent at handling electrical-system diagnosis and repair. Computers only exacerbate this situation for mechanics who have all to do to understand simple DC electricity, much less advanced computer electronics. Supposedly, "on-board diagnostics" makes up for mechanic ineptitude. The idea behind on-board diagnostics is that the computer monitors various system functions, and when it senses a malfunction it identifies the location of the problem. All the mechanic has to do is "read" the "failure codes" from the computer using a special piece of test equipment. Failure codes are numerical codes that pinpoint a particular defective part as the source of a performance problem. Theoretically, if your car doesn't start because of a bad ignition module the computer will record a corresponding error code indicating that the module is bad. Your mechanic just reads the code with his tester, replaces the defective module, and you're on your way. Not quite that simple!

Enamored with the high-tech mystique and promise of

computer precision built into their new cars, a lot of motorists are surprised when they experience great difficulty getting their dealers to resolve engine-performance complaints under warranty. When an engine conks out completely and just won't run at all, the computer may, and I stress may, record a specific failure code, making it easy for a mechanic to locate and replace the defective part. The going gets tougher when the engine trouble is intermittent, that is, when it doesn't happen all the time. For example, your car sometimes coughs and sputters on cold days until the engine fully warms up. Or once in a while it just won't start at all. So it's towed to the service department, and there it stays for a few days, after which you get it back, only to have the same thing happen all over again.

Why, the consumer asks, can't the dealer fix a car when the computer tells the mechanic what's wrong with it? In fact, the computer often can't identify many problems, especially the ones that occur intermittently. First of all, building on-board diagnostics into a computer system and related hardware is extremely expensive. Under pressure to keep new car prices competitive, auto manufacturers can only go so far in designing self-diagnostic capabilities into their cars. Secondly, there are many problems that can occur, which the computer does detect, but identifies as "intermittent code" failures. Codes of this nature tell the mechanic that the computer did "see" an abnormal signal coming from a particular component or group of components, but the abnormal indication was temporary.

For example, suppose your new car occasionally won't start when the weather is extremely cold. You bring it to the dealer and they find an intermittent failure code that suggests some prior malfunction in either the ignition module or the computer itself. A mechanic runs the standard tests recommended by the auto manufacturer and finds that the ignition module and the computer are now working normally, so they can't do anything about your problem. Well, isn't that just wonderful? They came to the brilliant conclusion that your car is now working fine. Of course, you told them at the outset that the problem was intermittent—sometimes it happens and sometimes it doesn't. The service manager may sympathize with you, but where is he going to get mechanics who have enough knowledge of computer electronics to go beyond the standard tests to diagnose your car's trouble? So, about all he can do is apologetically tell you to "come back if the problem recurs, and we'll take another look at it."

Thanks to the appearance of computers in newer model cars, more and more consumers are hearing this cop-out from dealer service departments. Again, it's something that shouldn't happen if a service manager knows what he is doing. Why should you as a consumer have to suffer because your dealer doesn't have the technical resources to differentiate between a bad ignition module and a failing computer? Why should you be persecuted because the factory might not pay the dealer if his mechanics replace both parts to ensure that your problem doesn't happen again? A good dealer will protect you from being victimized by bureaucratic rules imposed by the factory. All they have to do is replace both suspect parts with new ones, sabotage the old ones, and send them back to the factory for warranty reimbursement. Your problems are solved and the dealer gets paid by the factory.

Unfortunately, too many car buyers unsuspectingly do business with dealers whose service departments are not professionally managed. If you are one of them, you'll have to know how to properly present your complaints to the service manager to minimize your chances of getting the bum's rush instead of the warranty repairs you deserve. Actually, even if you have bought your car from a first-rate dealer, the suggestions I am about to give you are still worth following to protect your own interests.

How to Complain to the Service Manager

When your car isn't working as it should, be sure to accurately describe the symptoms to the people in the service department. If your car's engine won't start in very cold weather for example, don't merely say "the engine isn't running right." Be as precise as possible in conveying the exact nature of your complaint. The service manager or assistant will write a short description of the complaint as you have related it on a document called a repair order, or "RO" as they refer to it in the auto-repair business. The RO provides instructions to the mechanic, defining the nature of the malfunction symptoms in your car.

Before you sign the RO, check that the problem with your car has been accurately recorded on the document. You may be in a rush to leave the shop and get on with your business, but the attention to detail will be worth your effort. If the RO merely says "check engine performance/hard starting," the mechanic may not specifically check the components, which in his experience can cause *cold weather* starting trouble. After the mechanic has completed his examination of your car, the RO may be noted with the comment "Engine OK—no problem found." You'll undoubtedly be irritated over having left your car in the shop all day, only to discover that the mechanic who worked on it didn't really know the problem he was supposed to diagnose.

The Importance of Accurate Repair Records

There's another reason for insisting that the RO precisely define the nature of your complaint. It's important that you keep a record of every malfunction you bring to your dealer's attention while your vehicle is covered by its warranty. If you're doing business with a technically incompetent service department, or one that just doesn't want to do warranty work, they may stall you or postpone resolution of your problems until the warranty expires. Without a detailed account of your past complaints, you might not have grounds for demanding a warranty extension from the factory.

I've seen this kind of thing happen many times. A motorist hears an unusual noise coming from the engine and complains to the dealer. The service manager records the complaint on an RO with the expression "check engine." He then indicates the result as "OK." The customer complains a few more times, and in each case the RO is written the same way. After the warranty expires, the engine noise gets worse due to the failure of a wrist pin or a connecting rod bearing. Now the consumer feels vindicated about his suspicions—the engine was bad all along!

Armed with a few RO's, each containing the instruction "check engine," the consumer feels confident that there is sufficient documentation of prior complaints to justify demanding a warranty extension. Ah, but here comes the unpleasant surprise! "I wish I could help you Mr. Consumer," says the service manager, "but my hands are tied. You see, these RO's just talk about an engine-performance complaint, and we couldn't find anything wrong with the way your car ran, so no action was taken. If there was a problem inside the engine, we definitely would have repaired it under warranty. But now, we just don't have the authority to do that. But we can give you a factory rebuilt engine for about $3,800." Poor gullible Mr. Consumer has been ripped off by his dealer. And with no real evidence of prior complaints about engine noise, chances are the factory won't be too helpful either.

Even if you are fortunate enough to be doing business with a good service department worthy of your trust, you should still be vigilant about accurate complaint documentation. There are some problems that can occur with your automobile that don't seem to justify immediate corrective action. You may not even be too insistent about forcing the dealer to take action because you don't want to tie up your car in the shop if you can avoid it. A typical case could be an automatic transmission that takes a little too long to shift, or occasionally seems to slip just a bit. The dealer may check it out and genuinely believe there is no serious problem. Consequently, the RO may say "Check transmission and road test/no problem found. Transmission operates to specifications." If the transmission fails after the warranty expires, your ROs containing evidence of prior complaints can help the dealer get the factory to pay for a transmission overhaul.

Just a word of caution here. Just because you have ROs indicating a concern about transmission performance does not mean that you will be entitled to special consideration after your warranty expires. If push comes to shove with the factory, their position will be that your transmission worked to specifications when your car was road tested, so any failure must be attributed to a subsequent malfunction. To avoid this pitfall, make sure that your dealer doesn't simply note on your RO a comment such as "Transmission operates to specifications."

Get Documentation of Test Results

The service manager should include the road-test results of shift-point checks and any pressure tests that may have been done. Shift-point analysis entails recording the speeds at which the transmission shifts under various conditions. Pressure-test results provide an indication of hydraulic pressures in the transmission as indicated by test gauges. Some manufacturers recommend a stall test—a procedure in which engine speed is brought up to the maximum attainable rpms with the transmission in drive, but with the brakes locked so that the vehicle can't move. This kind of data is objective, and gives you a record of whether or not your transmission was really operating "to specifications" at the time it was road tested.

You must be suspicious of any service manager who is reluctant to give you such a report. Objective testing is absolutely necessary when there is any question about whether an automobile is genuinely performing to manufacturer's specifications. Incidentally, if you have some doubts about the integrity of the service department you are dealing with, demanding a written report of test results is an absolute must. You'll be surprised how your firmness on this issue will command respect, possibly to the extent that you might get decent warranty service from a shop that otherwise had no intentions of doing anything about your complaint. Too often, motorists are willing to accept "unit works normally," "no problem found," or "operating at specifications" as assurance that there's nothing to worry about. Without objective test results, such assurances could just be platitudes intended to placate a gullible consumer.

If you have any doubts about your dealer's thoroughness in carrying out appropriate tests to adequately diagnose your car, make a small investment in a copy of the manufacturer's shop manual, or see if your local library has one for your model. If your library doesn't have the manufacturer's manuals, general service manuals such as those produced by *Motor, Chilton*, and *Mitchell* are excellent alternatives, and most libraries have some of these on the shelves. In many instances, the manual will tell you what the suggested tests are to establish whether your car is really operating at specifications.

First, go to the *troubleshooting* section of the manual. Look up the problem you are experiencing and see what the manufacturer's test procedures are. Sometimes, these tests are fully described in the corresponding repair section of the manual. It's not important for you to understand the nature of the tests. You just have to know that they exist. If your dealer can't provide you with the test results described in the manual, chances are no tests were done. Expressing your awareness of this situation to the service manager could impress upon him that you're no pushover and could motivate him to take some serious action on your car. This is a far better strategy than waiting for a breakdown to occur and going into arbitration or legal action seeking compensation.

Of course, to brush you off, an unscrupulous service manager might read the normal test result specifications from the manual and record these on your repair order without having actually done the tests. To discourage this, visit the shop from time to time while your car is being serviced. Few service managers will bother to waste a lot of time on a charade with you hanging around the shop. The service manager would consider it easier to just give you what you want to get you off his back. Sometimes it pays to make a pest of yourself.

Another way to nudge a service manager into helping you out involves capitalizing on your knowledge of the warranty system. Keep in mind that few service managers you talk to will be as imaginative as they should in dealing with the factory. The burden may rest with you to suggest some of the creative ways your dealer's service manager can fix your car without undue concern about the potential for warranty-claim rejection. Just tactfully broach some of the possibilities previously discussed in this chapter, including sabotaging suspected bad parts. At the same time, try to temper your suggestions with a tone of sympathetic understanding of the problems he has dealing with the factory.

How to Avoid an Argument with the Service Manager

You must avoid sounding blatantly adversarial. For example, the threat of a lawsuit will not be well-received and could be counterproductive. These days, everybody in America is suing somebody, so the courts are overloaded and backlogged. Because of this, your car may be a pile of rusted scrap in a junkyard before you get your day in court. Your threat will, therefore, not be credible and will only inflame the situation. Instead, use diplomacy. Your knowledge of the service department's interactions with the factory regarding warranties will make a far stronger impression than the threat of litigation.

Based on my years in the car business, I've seen more than enough evidence of this to convince me that flagrant consumer hostility usually doesn't pay off. Once I was talking to the service manager in a large foreign-car dealership in Philadelphia when a disgruntled car owner screeched into the shop in a complete frenzy. The driver had bought the car brand-new just one day earlier. To his absolute disgust this paradigm of Italian technology equipped with four-wheel disc brakes stopped about as fast as Santa's sled on an ice pond. So it had some brake trouble! Is that anything to go nuts about?

To its incensed driver I suppose it was. He bolted out of the car and ran off into the showroom, his fists clenched, and shouting epithets about the owner of the dealership. Having met Umberto (the dealer principal) I knew the combination of his volatile temper and the aggressiveness shown by this hothead customer would make for quite a fireworks display. What ensued was a study in how a customer should *not* go about trying to persuade a dealer to fix his car under warranty.

Umberto and his enraged customer came storming into

the shop like a professional wrestling tag team anxious to get into the ring to tear up their opponents. The commotion was so loud that all other activity in the service department stopped short, with everyone's eyes focused on Umberto and his adversary. The customer loudly protested that he had been "screwed" by Umberto, who he believed had sold him a car that had not been properly checked out by the shop before it was delivered. Had a mechanic examined it, he asserted, the brake malfunction would have been detected. Once the obvious safety defect was noticed, the car would not have passed a state inspection. Therefore, the customer concluded, the inspection sticker must be immediately removed from the windshield and repairs initiated without delay.

At that, Umberto's customer became so agitated that he grabbed Umberto by the arm and dragged him toward the corner of the windshield where the inspection sticker was affixed, wildly pointing to the sticker, and insisting that Umberto get it off his car instantly and fix the brakes with no delay. Even from a distance I could see the blood vessels bulging in Umberto's brow as he reached his boiling point. Now the fuse was lit!

Umberto began shouting like a madman that he wasn't a mechanic and wouldn't fix anybody's car personally. I guess the mere suggestion that Umberto lower himself to getting his manicured hands dirty was just too demeaning to tolerate. In his characteristically broken English he went on the counterattack.

"Who the fucka you think you are to treata me lika some greasa monkey, you bastard?" screamed Umberto.

"I think you're a dumb Guinea crook," his tormentor replied, standing eyeball to eyeball like one kid challenging another for violating his turf.

"Geta you filthy nosa outa my face," warned Umberto.

"Then get that inspection sticker out of my car," answered the customer.

"You wanta you inspection sticker? Here I giva you the sticker."

At that Umberto ran over to a mechanic's tool box and seized a huge hammer. Seeing Umberto coming back toward the car brandishing this formidable weapon, the customer backed off. This made room for Umberto to approach the area of the windshield bearing the sticker, where he planted his legs firmly on the shop floor, and with one sweeping and dramatic swing, bashed out the glass with the hammer. Picking up the fragments bearing the remains of the inspection sticker, Umberto ran over to the startled customer and threw the pile of glass at him. With a look of scorn on his face, Umberto parted with the words: "You wanta the sticker, here's you sticker."

I won't go into the details of what transpired after that, but suffice it to say that the police got involved and it turned into quite a mess. After the smoke cleared, things got hot again as another unhappy customer stormed into the shop waving a repair order. She approached Victorio, the service manager, demanding that he lower the bill for repairs made on her car. Victorio, who spoke English rather eloquently, smugly told her that her bill was her bill and that was it. She came back with the comment: "What you people around here need is a little honesty." Unable to handle this affront to his integrity, Victorio replied: "Lady, what I need is a gun to shoot assholes like you. Now get the hell out of here and go tell your problems to Umberto." She was stopped on the way to the showroom by Victorio's assistant, who mercifully told her that it wasn't a good time for Umberto to be disturbed.

Let what happened in Umberto's dealership be a lesson to you about what can occur when you make the mistake of thinking that hostility is a viable substitute for diplomacy when expressing complaints about your car. People in the service business have to listen to a lot of woes all day long and they have a low threshold for patience. Smart consumers will use better strategies than shouting invectives to get what they want.

5

▼ ▼ ▼

How to Get Free Repairs After Your Car's Warranty Has Expired

After your car's warranty expires you may not have to pay to fix everything that goes wrong with it. If you know what you are doing, you can get the manufacturer to foot the bill for certain repairs without going through the hassles of arbitration or a lawsuit. Yes, there are effective ways to bargain with auto manufacturers for out-of-warranty financial assistance, or a "goodwill adjustment" as it is sometimes called. All you need is a little knowledge of how the system works.

Dealing with auto companies without this knowledge can be as frustrating as dealing with large government bureaucracies. It's not that the auto companies are as sinister as they are sometimes portrayed by certain consumer groups. Car manufacturers really do care about their products and their customers. However, like government agencies, the larger auto companies have many employees interpreting complicated internal policies and regulations. The result can be confusion and inconsistency in the way customers are treated. This holds true for owners of foreign as well as domestic cars. Don't imagine that the Japanese and Europeans are benevolent philanthropists—they're out to make a buck in the U.S. market, and they don't treat their customers any better than the domestic manufacturers do.

Whether you own a domestic or an imported car, you stand about the same chance of getting help from the factory if you have a problem after your car's warranty has expired. In either case, you can improve the odds if you know how the automobile bureaucracies work. With this knowledge you'll enhance your bargaining power and come away with the results you are looking for without the hassles of a lawsuit.

A good way to get familiar with the system is to take a look at the experiences others have had with it, and then apply what you have learned to your own circumstances. Once you know all the typical excuses car companies use to deny requests for out-of-warranty repairs, you should be able to avoid a lot of pitfalls and negotiate more intelligently on your own behalf.

Skelton Versus General Motors: Making the Factory Honor Its Warranty Obligations

In any discussion of how well consumers fare in their dealings with auto companies, one manufacturer is usually in the spotlight—General Motors. With all the GM bashing that goes on in the press, one could easily get the idea that this behemoth American auto company embodies all that is undesirable or unscrupulous about the way the factories treat their customers, especially those having problems after their vehicles' warranties have expired.

Actually, GM is the unfortunate target of so much bad publicity simply because it is so big. Having had direct experience tangling with GM as a consultant in one of the largest consumer class-action lawsuits ever successfully brought against a car manufacturer, I have some insight into the way the company treats its customers. In retrospect, I can see that GM was exceptionally fair to some customers who had legitimate grievances about their cars. At the same time, the company was exceptionally callous toward other customers who deserved much better treatment. The dichotomy in GM's attitude can only be explained by attributing it to quirks in its huge bureaucracy, not a premeditated conspiracy to cheat owners of GM cars out of the post-warranty repairs they deserved.

The lawsuit I'm referring to (Skelton v. General Motors, U.S. District Court, Northern District of Illinois. No. 79C1243) involved millions of GM cars built between 1976 and 1980 that were equipped with the THM-200 automatic transmission. Many of these transmissions failed at a relatively low mileage. The resultant rash of consumer complaints provoked inquiries and investigations by the Federal Trade Commission and various state agencies. The press was not easy on GM; nor were television newscasters. Readers and TV viewers became outraged at reports of GM's "ruthless stonewalling" and refusal to pay for repairs to THM-200 transmissions that failed. Complaints continued to mount, the outcome being the filing of a class-action lawsuit against GM on behalf of everyone who had ever purchased a vehicle equipped with the infamous transmission. A settlement of $17,000,000 was finally approved by the U.S. District Court on March 16, 1987.

A consortium of attorneys retained me as an expert to examine the evidence in the case and to provide technical advice. What I discovered was colossal bungling in the way GM handled its problems with the THM-200 automatic transmission. The errors the corporation committed in the way it treated its customers were actually no different from those committed by any other car company. In fact, the same things go on today, particularly in smaller auto companies, but the number of consumers affected is often not large enough to provoke any clamor. The little guys always get away with murder, figuratively speaking. Because of its size, GM just has to sneeze, and the whole automotive world catches cold.

Many thousands of motorists certainly got sick of their GM cars, thanks to the THM-200 transmission. Despite their appeals to GM for help, they were left out in the cold. They got some pretty flimsy excuses from some people at General Motors for not helping them. Such excuses are rather commonplace in the auto industry; they come from a standard menu of snow jobs that manufacturers give to disgruntled customers to brush them off. Customer relations people just recite from a script, trying to pacify unhappy consumers with one defense of the factory's untenable position after another, until they hit on one that works and gets them off their backs. Chances are, some day you'll hear a similar line if you request out-of-warranty financial consideration from the manufacturer of your car.

Here are some of the excuses GM came up with for denial of goodwill adjustments to plaintiffs in Skelton v. General Motors:

► We don't pay for repairs performed by any shop other than an authorized dealer.

► We can't pay for repairs because we didn't have the opportunity to inspect the parts in their failed condition on the vehicle.

► We can't help you with out-of-warranty assistance because you never complained about your car while it was under warranty.

► We can't help you with out-of-warranty assistance even though you registered a complaint under warranty, because your vehicle gave you thousands of trouble-free miles after your most recent complaint. This proves there was nothing wrong with it at the time you complained to the dealer.

► We can't help you with out-of-warranty assistance because you abused your car.

If these excuses are rules that prescribe how the factory should handle its customers, then the rules were made to be broken. And broken they were, over and over again, when General Motors' zone offices helped owners of THM-200 transmissions. Let's take a look at cases where GM chose to throw the rule book at certain customers, but made exceptions on behalf of others. You'll see how auto manufacturers typically deal with customer problems. You'll also gain the knowledge you'll need to get your own car problems solved when they come up. Apply what you learn, and you may be able to get your car repaired free even after its warranty expires.

Excuses Car Manufacturers Use to Avoid Helping Customers with Out-of-Warranty Repairs

EXCUSE NUMBER 1

"We Don't Pay for Repairs Performed by Any Shop Other Than an Authorized Dealer"

Have you ever heard that line before from a car company? Suppose that your car breaks down and requires emergency repairs. You get the car fixed at an independent repair shop, and subsequently complain to the factory that the breakdown occurred at an unacceptably low mileage. You can't believe that normal wear and tear could cause such a failure—there must have been some defect in manufacturing. But the factory doesn't see things your way. They refuse even to consider your protests and requests for financial assistance because you had your car fixed at other than a franchised dealer's service department.

Several of the plaintiffs in Skelton v. General Motors were given that excuse. One of them, Raymond Gruarin, complained to his Pontiac dealer while his car was under warranty that its transmission was noisy. According to Mr. Gruarin, a GM representative drove his car and pronounced it "normal." At 25,000 miles the transmission failed, at which time the dealer overhauled it at Mr. Gruarin's expense. At 31,000 miles it failed again. This time an independent mechanic rebuilt the transmission. Once again, Mr. Gruarin paid the bill.

Mr. Gruarin appealed in writing to Pontiac for financial assistance and got a reply from the Williamsville, New York, district office. The letter stated:

> We are unable to justify repairs made by other than a Pontiac dealership.

A similar denial was given to another plaintiff, Milo Madsen, whose THM-200 transmission failed at less than 21,000 miles. An independent repair shop replaced the original transmission, after which Madsen asked GM for monetary consideration. The Minneapolis zone office of the Chevrolet Motor division gave him this answer:

> Since your vehicle is beyond the terms of the manufacturer's warranty and was repaired by

other than a Chevrolet dealer, we are unable to consider your request and cannot be of assistance to you in this matter.

BENDING THE RULES

Exceptions to Excuse Number 1

William Fehrenbach had his THM-200 transmission rebuilt at 26,000 miles by an independent shop at a cost of $383.76. Thereafter, he wrote to GM seeking a reimbursement. Three months later he got a check from Chevrolet Motor Division for $383.76.

William King spent $593.07 to have an independent repair shop overhaul his THM-200 transmission when it was 12 months beyond the expiration of the warranty. He was lucky enough to get at least a partial reimbursement from Chevrolet Division in the sum of $163.75.

What to Do If Your Car's Manufacturer Hits You with Excuse Number 1

As hard-nosed as GM is reputed to be, the corporation displayed remarkable generosity to certain owners of THM-200 transmissions, absorbing all or part of the cost of repairs done by other than authorized GM service facilities. As a regional service manager with two auto manufacturers, I have personally authorized reimbursements to some consumers under similar circumstances, and I've heard of numerous other cases in which this was done.

You shouldn't assume, though, that any manufacturer

will be so generous with you, unless there are extenuating circumstances. If you incur a repair bill at an independent shop because it is impractical to utilize the services of an authorized dealer, the factory may respond favorably to your request for out-of-warranty financial assistance. Of course, the decision will depend in part on whether or not there has been an exceptionally high incidence of problems of the kind you have had with your car.

Even if you are initially turned down, you have reason to be persistent if the factory's excuse is predicated on a rationale analogous to the one GM offered Pontiac owner Raymond Gruarin, namely:

> We are unable to justify repairs made by other than a Pontiac dealership.

In fact, every car manufacturer can and does justify repairs made by other than franchised dealers under the *sublet work* system. Quite often, a dealer does not have the facilities to handle certain kinds of repairs, and will therefore subcontract the work to an independent shop. The auto manufacturers knowingly pay for this sublet work under warranty.

For example, one plaintiff in the THM-200 litigation, Sue Shubert, was billed $486.20 by a Chevrolet dealer for a transmission overhaul. The dealer's records indicated that the work was sublet, that is, the transmission was actually repaired by an independent shop. Nevertheless, Chevrolet was kind enough to arrange a 50 percent reimbursement for Shubert.

If a manufacturer refuses to assist you because you had your car fixed by an independent shop, let the experience of Sue Shubert and thousands of others like her provide encouragement for you to be tenacious in your efforts to get financial help from the factory. Make the manufacturer aware that you know about the sublet work system and precedents for goodwill payments under circumstances similar to yours. You might be surprised how fast the factory changes its tune! Auto manufacturers often get gun-shy when it comes to taking on consumers who know the inner workings of the business.

EXCUSE NUMBER 2

"We Can't Pay for Repairs Because We Didn't Have the Opportunity to Inspect the Parts in Their Failed Condition on the Vehicle."

This is the line you might get when you have your car fixed out-of-warranty, and retain the old parts for factory inspection. Later, you appeal to the factory for help and they turn thumbs down to your request because the parts could not be examined by a factory representative as they were being removed from the vehicle.

Mr. Jerry Nirenberg had his THM-200 transmission overhauled at 14,950 miles by an independent repair shop. He later took the parts removed from his transmission to a Chevrolet dealer for inspection by a GM representative, hoping to get compensated for his out-of-pocket expenses for the overhaul. GM never did look at his parts. Instead, Nirenberg received a letter from the Tarrytown, New York, Chevrolet zone office containing the following statement:

We do not of course discredit the competence of the facility that repaired your vehicle; however,

since we have been denied the opportunity to examine the parts in their failed condition on the vehicle, we are not in a position to make a decision
regarding our responsibility in this matter.

Scott Reid's THM-200 transmission required an overhaul at 16,497 miles. Although work was done by an independent shop, the old parts were retained. Reid
offered to make the parts available to GM for inspection
pursuant to his request for financial assistance. The Cin-
cinnati zone office of the Chevrolet Motor Division answered as follows:

We do not of course discredit the competence of
the facility that repaired your vehicle; however,
since we have been denied the opportunity to examine the parts in their failed condition on the vehicle, we are not in a position to make a decision
regarding our responsibility in this matter.

Obviously Nirenberg and Reid got the official company
line from Chevrolet. Or was it so official? Consider what
happened to Bruce Davis, a Chevrolet owner who paid
for a transmission overhaul at 19,283 miles.

BENDING THE RULES

Exceptions to Excuse Number 2

Davis had his transmission overhauled by an independent repair shop. After he wrote to GM asking for
financial assistance, he got this reply from Chevrolet's
central office in Detroit, dated July 3, 1979:

From the details supplied in your correspondence of recent date, we note your 1977 Chevrolet Impala is no longer covered by the Chevrolet new vehicle warranty. Consequently, it is doubtful any adjustment can be made for the repairs you had done at Cottman Transmission.

In order to properly establish if Chevrolet does have any responsibility to you for the repairs in question, we feel we should be afforded an opportunity to see the damaged parts in question. Under the circumstances, our recommendation would be for you to take the damaged parts to an authorized Chevrolet dealer. Since Chevrolet dealers do not have the authority to make the decision on an over warranty repair, he can tag the parts for inspection by a field representative from Chevrolet, and on his next visit to the dealer, the field representative can determine whether an adjustment can be made.

So what happened to the requirement that parts be examined in their failed state on the vehicle? Davis was led to believe that all that was necessary to be considered for a goodwill adjustment was that his transmission parts be made available for examination by a GM representative. And this determination was made at Chevrolet's central office in Detroit, not a local zone office.

Unfortunately for Davis, the suggestions originating in Detroit were not followed at the local level. In a subsequent correspondence Davis noted:

I was finally contacted by the [Chevrolet] field representative in the first week of November 1979. This hearing that I was granted was by phone. No meeting was scheduled, no advance notice was given and he did not need to avail himself of the opportunity to see the parts which GM requested in the July 3 letter.

I was further informed that GM was not responsible, that I was unlucky but OUT. He expressed his "sincere sympathy" and hoped that I would not hold this bad experience against GM products.

There were many plaintiffs in the THM-200 litigation who received some financial assistance from General Motors without the need for an inspection of the failed transmission parts in their so-called failed condition on the vehicle. Indeed, the aforementioned letter from Chevrolet's central office suggests that high-level corporate policy leaned toward the more sensible position of willingness to evaluate failed transmission parts well after repairs had been made. Unfortunately, good sense at command headquarters didn't always prevail in the trenches, to the detriment of thousands of GM car owners.

What to Do If Your Car's Manufacturer Hits You with Excuse Number 2

If an auto manufacturer begs off from helping you because the parts in question cannot be examined "in their failed state on the vehicle," what they're really telling you is "we don't believe that the old parts you have really came from your vehicle." There are some circumstances under which an examination of failed parts as they are disassembled after removal makes sense. In most cases however, the cause of failure can be determined by an inspection of the components after they have been removed. General Motors knows this, and so does every other auto manufacturer.

Consider for example, what happened to Charles Sabin, a plaintiff in the THM-200 litigation. Sabin's car experienced two transmission failures, one at 22,000 miles and another at 26,000 miles. Disgusted, he contacted the Rockville, Maryland, zone office of Pontiac Motor Division seeking reimbursement. Note Pontiac's reply pertaining to parts inspection:

> If, however, you still have in your possession the original failed components, please advise us accordingly. We will certainly review failure to determine probable cause.

So much for the need to examine parts in their failed condition on the vehicle. But what about the nature of the examination itself? If your car's manufacturer agrees to examine parts and then renders a decision against you, can you consider their judgment reliable? Can you depend on a competent, technically authoritative opinion? The answer is sometimes yes, but often no. What you will frequently run into is a perfunctory, superficial examination of parts designed to placate you or to justify a predetermined decision to give you nothing.

This was true in the case of Arthur Jacobsen, a plaintiff in Skelton v. General Motors. Jacobsen's THM-200 burned out at 12,444 miles and was repaired by a Chevrolet dealer at Jacobsen's expense, even though he had complained about the transmission's performance on three previous occasions before the warranty had expired. A Chevrolet factory representative inspected the transmission parts and refused to offer financial assistance on the grounds that the parts inspection had indicated driver abuse.

Mr. Jacobsen had occasionally used his car to tow a small trailer. The GM representative considered this abusive. Interestingly, Jacobsen's car required major engine work at 2,264 miles, but at that time no issue was raised about the adverse effects of trailer towing, and repairs were made under warranty. With the car's odometer indicating 444 miles over the nominal 12,000-mile warranty limit, trailer-towing suddenly became an issue!

The factory representative seized upon this as an excuse to deprive Jacobsen of out-of-warranty aid, claiming that, based on his examination of the parts, towing the trailer contributed to burn-out of the transmission friction clutches. Regarding this opinion, in a report I wrote, which was later submitted to the U.S. District Court for the Northern District in Illinois, I made the following observations:

> Even considering that towing excessive weight could under certain circumstances contribute to premature transmission failure, this doesn't mean that it is always a factor. It would be interesting to review the scientific technique [the Chevrolet representative] utilized during his inspection of Jacobsen's transmission parts to differentiate between friction material failures due to trailer towing, and the various failures caused by the many THM-200 defects that have been known to induce such failures.
>
> In section 1A of this report it was noted that plaintiff Hans Kull experienced transmission failure involving friction material, at a much higher mileage than Jacobsen. GM paid for Kull's repairs, thereby not alleging abuse of the transmission by Kull. In addition to the implicit conclusion that driver abuse need not be present to

cause THM-200 friction material failure, Kull's situation vis-à-vis Jacobsen's might lead one to conclude that GM is not unwilling to seize upon an excuse to avoid responsibility for certain product failures, if such an excuse is conveniently available. In Jacobsen's case it was.

Another THM-200 owner experienced a similarly dubious parts inspection. Clifford McIntee purchased a Chevrolet as a dealer demo, with a GM warranty extended to 17,100 miles from the nominal 12,000 miles. At 12,672 miles the transmission failed and was overhauled by a GM dealer. At 20,158 miles the transmission failed again, at which time it was removed and disassembled for inspection at an authorized GM dealer. A factory representative inspected the failed parts and refused to accept any responsibility for the cost of the repairs. Disappointed with the decision, McIntee had the car towed to an independent transmission shop, where it was fixed at his expense. Later he appealed to the Chevrolet Motor Division from which he received this answer:

> The parts removed from your transmission were inspected by A. E. Lucas, Area Service Manager, who could not find any indication of a defect.

In my report filed in U.S. District Court, I made these observations about the Chevrolet area service manager's findings:

> In this case, GM did not accuse McIntee of abusing the transmission as it had done with Jacobsen. The reason for denial of goodwill adjustment was that no defects could be found in the failed parts.

It seems surprising that the transmission only
lasted about 8,000 miles subsequent to the first
overhaul. A defect-free transmission might reasonably be expected to last longer than that.
It is very doubtful that Mr. A. E. Lucas could
have reached his conclusion based on substantive
technical examinations. To say that parts are defect-free requires that they be carefully measured
and the readings compared to blueprint specifications.

This would be necessary minimally, to determine that parts are not dimensionally defective.
Other more complex tests, some requiring the use
of laboratory equipment, would be necessary to
detect certain subtle defects that could result in
functional anomalies. Since representatives of automobile companies such as Mr. Lucas don't routinely in their travels carry blueprints or sophisticated test equipment, it is improbable that Mr.
Lucas' decision regarding McIntee's parts was
anything other than arbitrary in its basis.

Regarding the parts that were replaced on Mr.
McIntee's transmission, the report went on to say:

Regarding the actual repairs, it is interesting to
note that during the overhaul done by the GM
dealer at 12,672 miles, one part, #8628206 rear
sun gear, was replaced. The repair receipt outlin-
ing the parts replaced during the second overhaul
lists once again one #8628206 rear sun gear. Presumably Mr. A. E. Lucas would have believed
that this part was defective the first time, but not
defective the second time. However, two replacements in a 20,158 mile period hardly seems coinci-

dental. Indeed, McIntee received less than 8,000 trouble-free miles from the initially replaced sun gear.

The bottom line here for you, the consumer, is that you should not place too much credence in visual inspections of your car's failed parts by factory representatives when these inspections are performed in a dealer's service department. Their decisions can frequently be hasty and arbitrary. Rarely do they perform accurate measurements and comparisons with specifications to arrive at their conclusions. More often they'll render impromptu judgments based more on the mood they're in and budgetary considerations than scientific method.

This places you at an extreme disadvantage in getting your car's problems resolved, especially where difficult-to-diagnose malfunctions are concerned. Routine breakdowns that occur commonly lend themselves to snap judgments—cause and effect is pretty clear cut. Consequently, it's easy for the factory to assess its liability and determine its willingness to help you in out-of-warranty situations. But when your car has a problem that is out of the ordinary, a lot of time may be needed to determine the cause. Extensive tests may be necessary and parts might require extremely precise scrutiny. All too often though, the factory representative and the dealer may be unwilling to spend enough time to investigate the defect. Instead, they'll take the easy way out and blame the malfunction on driver abuse. Or, they'll tell you that there's nothing wrong with your car—the problem is just your imagination.

Many of the plaintiffs in the THM-200 litigation were subjected to this kind of evasive treatment. One, James Chvala, experienced difficulties with his transmission at 11,000 miles. He described the problem as a:

hesitation in starting up and [it] would skip the low gear trains and jump ahead in high gear with severe strain on the whole transmission.

Later, Chvala further elaborated on the nature of the transmission's unusual performance:

> . . . this transmission would hesitate when we wanted to start forward motion—it would just sit still—as a result, we would increase our accelerator pressure, then without warning the car would jump forward . . .

A Chevrolet dealer overhauled the transmission's valve body under warranty in an attempt to correct the problem. The valve body is basically a collection of hydraulic control valves that direct the flow of fluid in the transmission to determine what gear it is in.

While driving home from the dealership in his supposedly repaired car, the rear wheels locked up, causing the drive shaft to break and resulting in other extensive damage to the vehicle. A Chevrolet factory representative looked at Chvala's car and refused to authorize financial assistance, asserting that Chvala had thrown the transmission into reverse while driving at a 40 mile per hour forward speed. Apparently, the fact that the transmission failure occurred just after the valve body had been overhauled was deemed a coincidence.

When I reviewed Chvala's files, I didn't think it was a coincidence at all. When the valve body is removed from a THM-200 transmission, as it was from Chvala's car, a manual detent roller and spring assembly is also removed. This part functions to keep the transmission manual valve in the position selected by the driver, that is, it keeps the transmission from shifting out of gear upon hitting a bump. If the bolt that secures the manual detent roller and spring assembly is not tightened properly when the valve body is installed, it is possible for the manual valve to change position unexpectedly, possibly causing the transmission to engage reverse gear while driving forward.

A letter subsequently sent to Chvala by the Chevrolet central office in Detroit (denying him any further assistance) made no mention of this possibility. It could be assumed then, that the condition of the manual detent roller and spring assembly was not checked by the GM representative. When I reviewed this situation I found the lack of inquisitiveness on GM's part surprising, especially in consideration of Chvala's prior complaint that "this transmission would hesitate when we wanted to start forward motion—it would just sit still."

Apparently the Chevrolet factory representative considered this a coincidence in relation to the subsequent transmission failure. My review of the files of 91 plaintiffs in Skelton v. General Motors revealed that at least 11 percent of them had complained about a similar malfunction of their transmission, which, in my report, I referred to as the "delayed drive syndrome." Even more of them may have had the same problem but did not voice concern about it because of more urgent worries about their transmissions. If anything could not be termed coincidental, it was the frequency of complaint about the "delayed drive syndrome." Could General Motors have been unaware of it?

Judging from the way some of the plaintiffs in the lawsuit were treated, more than a few people in the corporation were not aware of the condition. A case in point— Maurice Atzrodt. With 777 miles on his Chevrolet, Atzrodt took his new car back to the selling dealer, complaining that it sometimes failed to engage in drive. This erratic transmission performance manifested itself in cold weather. The service writer wrote instructions on the repair order to the mechanic to "check delay in trans—when putting in drive." Only some additional fluid was added as a corrective measure.

Three weeks later Atzrodt returned to the dealer with the same complaint. This time they noted on the repair order: "Trans—when in drive takes a while to move." The resolution of the complaint? "No trouble found" was written on the repair order. Ten days later the scenario was repeated and once again the transmission was declared "OK."

Finally, at 2,120 miles the dealer acceded to Atzrodt's demand that "exploratory surgery" be done on his transmission to get to the bottom of its peculiar behavior. According to Atzrodt, upon disassembling the unit, the mechanic expressed amazement that it had functioned at all, considering the extent of its internal damage. What particularly surprised the mechanic was that the transmission fluid was not burnt, an observation noted on the repair order. Typically, where a severe automatic transmission malfunction is evident, it is often accompanied by burnt fluid, an indicator of excessive slippage of the friction elements (clutches and bands).

Atzrodt was lucky that he had been doing business with a dealer who aggressively pursued a diagnosis of his car's problem even though it seemed to operate normally when a mechanic road tested it. Too often a customer is dismissed as a nut under these circumstances and nothing further is done. Fortunately for Atzrodt, the dealer believed his account of the "delayed drive syndrome."

Jack Hooke was not so fortunate. In early October, when the weather is relatively warm on Long Island, a transmission overhaul was done on Hooke's car. When the cold winds of January blew in, things changed as Hooke's Oldsmobile began to suffer from the "delayed drive syndrome.'' A telephone call to General Motors in Detroit requesting help got this written response from Oldsmobile's central office:

> With regards to the transmission in your vehicle, we have received a report from our Tarrytown Zone Office, which serves the dealers in your area. They inform us that Mr. R. D. Moye, District Service Manager operating out of that office, road tested your vehicle in November. . . . He felt your car was operating within Oldsmobile's specifications. Since he is technically trained and has the knowledge to make evaluative decisions of this type, we regret that Oldsmobile will be unable to modify your transmission for you.

A lot could have happened to Hooke's car between November, when Mr. Moye road tested it, and January, when Hooke called General Motors. Even assuming that the transmission previously functioned normally, the Oldsmobile District Service Manager might have been a bit curious about Hooke's latest problems, which he described in a letter to General Motors in Detroit:

> These past few weeks about 5 or 6 times now, I have backed my car out of my garage in the morning and my car would not shift into Drive Gear. The handle and indicator showed it was in drive but when I put the gas pedal down the motor raced like it was in neutral. I went back to my Olds dealer telling him that this transmission was failing and told him the symptoms. He asked me to leave it overnight to see if it would happen the next morning. The next morning it didn't happen

for him and he 'test drove' it with me. He ex-
claimed 'Look it shifts into high at 28 MPH. That's
perfect!' (Last year 22 MPH was perfect.)

Detroit's response to Hooke's letter?

Since it sells cars nationwide, Oldsmobile must of
necessity rely on its field service organization for
reports with regards to customers' product difficulties. We regret any misunderstanding that has
occurred with regard to a contact between you
and our Tarrytown Zone Office, and are referring
your latest correspondence back to that office.
Any further clarification with regard to your vehicle's shifting difficulties will come from either that
office or dealership personnel.

No further clarification was forthcoming. Hooke got
stuck in bureaucratic mud and was just spinning his
wheels trying to get any help locally from Oldsmobile.
Apparently Oldsmobile didn't have enough technical cu-
riosity about Hooke's transmission problems to devote
the time or energy to isolating the cause.

Another Long Island resident, Ellen Scroggins, ran into
the same indifference to the "delayed drive syndrome" in
her dealings with Pontiac. Purchased in January, the car
exhibited unusual transmission performance from the
start. On the same day she bought her new Grand Prix,
she returned it to her Pontiac dealer complaining about a
"slip in the transmission."

Subsequently, several attempts were made to fix the
transmission, including the replacement of a part called a
valve body spacer plate, with the new spacer plate bearing the number 8630574. The repair attempts failed. Out

of frustration, Scroggins wrote to General Motors in Detroit, asking for help. She got this reply:

> Our District Service Manager notified this office that . . . upon his test drive the transmission operated normally. Mr. Weiser [the District Service Manager] also offered to switch your transmission into his vehicle as he was that secure with its operation.

It is curious that Mr. Weiser felt that Scroggins's transmission was operating normally, since it had a critical part in it that made it impossible for it to shift according to specifications. The valve body spacer plate part number 8630574 was designed for use in an earlier model Grand Prix. It differed from the correct spacer plate numbered 8630561 in that it had a substantially larger governor-feed orifice, a drilled hole that affects governor pressure in the transmission and therefore the speed at which the transmission shifts. Scroggins's transmission could not have been operating to specifications with an incorrect part in it. Upon overhauling the transmission at a later date, a different dealer noticed the incorrect spacer plate and replaced it with the one designed for Scroggins's car.

Even after the overhaul, the "delayed drive syndrome" persisted, according to Scroggins. Was she exaggerating or was the transmission in fact defective? I had the opportunity to road test the car myself in December, with the temperature hovering around 15°F. The Grand Prix had been parked in Scroggins's driveway overnight. After starting the engine, I put the transmission in reverse and backed out. When I shifted into Drive, nothing happened—the car would not move. It did move forward in "L2" and "L1," but when placed in Drive, the transmission spontaneously disengaged several times while coasting to a stop. After four minutes of driving, the problem disappeared. Not exactly sterling performance from a transmission a Pontiac representative felt so confident in that he was willing to have it installed in his own car! Later, when I checked the fluid, it appeared perfectly normal, with no evidence of burning.

Obviously Scroggins and others like her had gotten a raw deal. Her transmission was in fact defective, yet Pontiac was unwilling to do anything about it. General Motors in Detroit sometimes showed more interest in blindly supporting the decisions of its local zone offices than resolving nagging technical difficulties with its cars. And the difficulties were resolvable.

Instead of getting bogged down in useless debates with customers about the alleged competence of its field organization, General Motors could have pursued more productive technical solutions. And where the THM-200 transmission was concerned, there were plenty of options. If there were any doubts about the veracity of the customers who complained about the operation of their cars in cold weather, local GM service personnel could have rented an environmental test facility. In an environmental chamber, the air temperature can be lowered (or raised) to the desired level, and the vehicle can be evaluated under conditions similar to those described by the customer. An even less complicated solution would have been merely to give new transmissions to customers as needed, and later examine the defective transmissions at a factory test facility.

Unfortunately for many THM-200 owners, General Motors chose to fall back on the results of dubiously conducted road tests, parts inspections, and assertions that their transmissions were performing "to specifications." Was this a corporate ploy to get disgruntled customers of their back? Not likely. Sloppy technical procedure was more probably a zone-level problem, not a national conspiracy originating in Detroit. Some owners of GM cars were treated quite fairly by their dealers, such as Maurice Atzrodt, whose dealer disassembled and later repaired his transmission even though initial examinations showed no evidence of a defect.

What happened to Atzrodt underscores both the need for thoroughness in evaluating a customer's complaints, and the favorable results consumers can get from a dealer when they are persistent. Atzrodt believed his transmission was defective and stuck to his guns until he got what he wanted. You should, too, if you have a problem with your car and have trouble making your dealer or the factory believe the malfunction is real.

Don't allow them to give you the bum's rush. As you have seen from the THM-200 owners' experiences, factory representatives cannot be relied upon to check out a car's problems objectively in every case. Road tests can be subjective. Parts can be given a cursory look and declared "normal" without accurate tests and measurements.

If you feel that you have not received a fair appraisal of your car's defects, write to the factory and demand an explanation of how their representative reached his decision. Insist that they check your car out under conditions that simulate those under which you experience problems. Demand manufacturing blueprints and specifications so that you can have an independent mechanic or machinist measure the parts in question and check them against factory standards. Get independent corroboration of your car's performance abnormalities so that you cannot easily be dismissed as a chronic complainer. Chances are the factory will fix your car rather than risk a legal confrontation.

EXCUSE NUMBER 3

*"We Can't Help You with Out-of-Warranty
Assistance Because You Never Complained
About Your Car When It Was Under Warranty."*

Frequently the artful dodgers in the automobile service industry attempt to bamboozle car owners with the story that if any defects are present in a car they will manifest themselves during the warranty period. So, if your car falls apart after the warranty expires, it couldn't be because of defective parts that were slowly failing while the warranty was in force.

That's the hogwash General Motors gave THM-200 owner Gertrude Gilson when she asked for financial assistance with her burned-out transmission. Responding to a letter from Gilson's attorney, General Motors' general counsel had this to say:

> . . . records of the Oldsmobile Division do not indicate that work was performed on the transmission under the Oldsmobile warranty. If you can provide documentation or other support for a mechanical problem with the transmission within the initial period of ownership, we will request the Oldsmobile Division to review this matter.

Gilson insisted that she did complain about the transmission when the warranty was in force. But she had no written records to prove it. Nor did plaintiff Joseph Henry, whose transmission failed at 28,760 miles. His appeal to GM for financial assistance got the following reply:

> Chevrolet Motor Division feels if a manufacturing defect is present, it will become apparent well within the liberal warranty limitations.

That's pure poppycock! The assertion that manufacturing defects always manifest themselves through malfunction symptoms within a certain number of miles is technically beyond substantiation. Besides, some owners of GM cars equipped with the THM-200 transmission who didn't complain about a problem while the warranty was in force were given financial assistance after its expiration.

BENDING THE RULES

Exceptions to Excuse Number 3

Several plaintiffs involved in the THM-200 class-action lawsuit received goodwill adjustments after their warranties had expired, even though none of them had previously complained about a transmission problem. Astonishingly, one plaintiff, Deborah Chrzanowski, bought her car *used* from its original owner. At the time, the vehicle had 17,000 miles on it, 5,000 miles over the 12,000-mile warranty. As far as Chrzanowski knew, the original owner never had any transmission trouble.

When the unit burned out at 18,909 miles, it was repaired by a Chevrolet dealer. Chrzanowski contacted the Chevrolet zone office hoping GM would foot the bill. Later, she received a goodwill check in the sum of

$119.68. Apparently, this time Chevrolet didn't feel that "if a manufacturing defect is present, it will become apparent well within the liberal warranty limitations."

The evidence indicates that Buick Division wasn't bound by such outrageous dogma either. When Verbinia Rodgers's Buick Regal broke down because of transmission failure, her pleas for help found a benevolent ear at the Buick zone office. The Buick factory representative paid for the entire cost of the repair less $100 that Rodgers absorbed herself.

What to Do If Your Car's Manufacturer Hits You with Excuse Number 3

The argument that you are not entitled to out-of-warranty assistance because you have no record of a complaint under warranty just doesn't hold water. This kind of cop-out is generally the fabrication of people at the zone office level, and does not typically represent corporate service policy.

However, if the manufacturer wants to save some money by not helping you out, this excuse could work because a lot of gullible consumers buy it, blaming themselves for not asking for documentation of their complaints. The manufacturer figures that if you have no documentation, you probably never registered a complaint. The gamble is that the liars will back off and drop the issue.

If you're not a liar and really believe in your cause, pierce through the factory's smoke screen about documentation, and focus on technical issues. What is responsible for the problem in your car? Could it be the result of a pre-existing condition? Can the factory state unequivocally that the problem was not developing while the warranty was in effect?

Ask for relevant service bulletins from the factory to see if they are aware of similar problems occurring with the same model cars as yours. If the problem is widespread, chances are you'll get help even though your warranty has expired. Ford and General Motors provide many of their service bulletins to the public upon request. To get service bulletins from Ford, call them at (800) 241-3673. Have your model year and vehicle identification number ready, along with a description of the part of the car you are concerned with (e.g., engine, air conditioning, power steering, etc.). Ask them if they have bulletins pertaining to that area of the car. General Motors will send you an index of the bulletins they have available by calling them at (800) 551-4123.

If you run into a snag getting bulletins from Ford, GM, or any other manufacturer, you can get them from the United States government through the National Highway Traffic Safety Administration (NHTSA). Write to:

National Highway Traffic Safety Administration
Technical Reference Library, Room 5108
400 Seventh Street S.W.
Washington, DC 20590

Ask for the service bulletins pertaining to the part of the car you are interested in. If you would rather call NHTSA, contact the technical reference library at (202) 366-2768. The technical reference library can make available a computer printout of all bulletins they have on file. From the printout you can select the bulletins of interest to you and order them from the library. If you have any trouble getting through to the technical reference library, contact the consumer liaison office at (202) 366-5971 or the office of public affairs at (202) 366-9550.

EXCUSE NUMBER 4

"We Can't Help You with Out-of-Warranty Assistance Even Though You Registered a Complaint under Warranty, Because Your Vehicle Gave You Thousands of Trouble-free Miles after Your Most Recent Complaint. This Proves There Was Nothing Wrong with It When You Complained to the Dealer."

Notice that this is a variation of excuse number 3. If the consumer can produce documentation of complaints while the warranty was in force, the next clever dodge is to call out the reserves—excuse number 4! Sure you complained about a problem under warranty. But if a problem really existed, why did your car operate thousands of miles before it finally broke down? Sorry, Charlie, we can't help you.

If the logic behind excuse number 4 sounds a little convoluted, think about how plaintiff James Owen felt when he got a letter from Chevrolet's Baltimore zone office containing this denial of his request for assistance:

> According to [the dealer's] repair orders #120460 and #16421 with 6,191 and 11,767 miles respectively on your vehicle, Chevrolet Motor Division must concur with their opinion, which was indicated on these repair orders as "okay" and "nor-

mal" in regard to the operation of the transmission, in view of the fact that the vehicle operated
for an additional 9,879 miles.

So, after having voiced his concerns about unusual
transmission behavior at 6,191 miles and 11,767 miles,
Owen was faced with a $545.80 transmission overhaul bill
at 21,646 miles. And Chevrolet Division had no interest in
picking up the tab. Just how reasonable was their position? In my report made available to the U.S. District
Court I made these observations about Owen's case:

The assertion that Owen's transmission was free
of defects at 11,767 miles in view of its additional
9,879 miles of useful life thereafter is patently absurd. The reality of the transmission's failure at
21,646 miles does more to raise doubts about [the
dealer's] diagnostic thoroughness than it does to
imply that the transmission was fine 9,879 miles
earlier. In fact, there is good reason to believe that
[the dealer] did not adequately test Owen's transmission. General Motors' service manuals prescribe a transmission pressure test procedure
which is useful in appraising the condition of the
oil pump and other internal components. In many
cases, the test procedure could detect impending
transmission failures that some technicians could
not predict on the basis of information gained
from a road test alone. Interestingly, Owen's oil
pump failed. However, there is no indication on
the repair document that a pressure test was performed on either occasion that Owen complained
to [the dealer].

The dealer did not adequately test the transmission and Chevrolet Division did nothing to rectify the mistake. Compounding the injustice done to Owen was the fact that some of the parts that failed in his transmission had been frequently failing in many other THM-200s. These parts were the subject of service bulletins about design changes to improve longevity. Could the Chevrolet Baltimore zone office have really believed that Owen's transmission was not in the process of self-destructing while its warranty was in force?

BENDING THE RULES

Exceptions to Excuse Number 4

I don't think they could have. And I certainly don't think that sort of lunacy reflected official General Motors corporate philosophy. Out of 91 files I reviewed in depth, I found five vehicles that had accumulated anywhere from 11,000 to 17,000 extra miles after the last transmission complaint had been registered, and in each of these cases, GM did not consider the extra mileage as evidence that the transmissions were working normally to begin with. In fact, all of these fortunate owners received goodwill compensation from GM to offset the cost of repairs.

What to Do If Your Car's Manufacturer Hits You with Excuse Number 4

Excuse number 4 is one of the most frivolous excuses an auto manufacturer might use to discourage you from further pursuing compensation for your out-of-warranty problems. To combat this nonsense, demand to see evidence of the tests performed (and the results) that formed the basis for the determination that your car was functioning normally when you last complained about it.

Relate this analogy to the factory representative who insulted you with a flimsy justification for refusing a goodwill adjustment. Every mechanic knows an engine can run for tens of thousands of miles with a knock in it before it blows up. But that doesn't mean it's operating normally until the shrapnel starts to fly!

Also, follow the same suggestions offered in connection with excuse number 3. Knowledge is power. Once you start flexing your muscles the factory will back off and peddle their balderdash to weaker prey.

EXCUSE NUMBER 5

"We Can't Help You with Out-of-Warranty Assistance Because You Abused Your Car."

The allegation of driver abuse is a favorite option in the factory's repertoire of stories concocted to justify not helping owners with their out-of-warranty problems. If the factory turns you down arbitrarily, chances are you'll be incensed. But if they can come up with some evidence that makes a driver-abuse theory plausible, then you might humbly drop your demand for help and contritely swear to treat your next car a little better.

Previously in this chapter I related the story of Chevrolet owner James Chvala who was accused of abusing his car while it was under warranty. The factory representative claimed that Chvala had thrown the transmission into reverse while cruising forward at 40 mph. However, only hours before it failed, the transmission had been worked on by a Chevrolet dealer. What happened to Chvala's car could have been the result of negligence on the part of the mechanic who fixed it. Even barring negligence, there are other alternatives to abuse as an explanation for what happened to Chvala's transmission. In fact, in just about every case of vehicle component failure I have ever investigated, there have been plausible theories other than abuse to explain the condition of the parts in question.

As I pointed out in the report filed with U.S. District Court:

> Unless a vehicle is severely and conspicuously accident damaged, it is virtually impossible to assign blame for premature automatic transmission failure to anything the operator could have done wrong, because the manifestations of such alleged abuse can be explained by numerous other causes. The one exception of course is a vehicle obviously modified for use on a race track. In such a case, abnormal use and even abuse is presumed.

BENDING THE RULES

Exceptions to Excuse Number 5

Getting stuck in snow is generally considered one of the most abusive things that can happen to a car as far as its automatic transmission is concerned. Nevertheless, Pontiac Grand Prix owner Bessie Jones, whose car got stuck in snow, was not accused of abusing it when the transmission failed at 3,784 miles. The dealer noted on the repair order "got stuck in snow" and proceeded to perform the necessary repairs free of charge.

Subsequently, the transmission failed again at 15,654 miles, at which time Jones asked General Motors to pay for the repairs. GM offered to absorb 50 percent of the cost provided work was done by a GM dealer, an offer Jones declined. Noteworthy is the fact that GM was generous enough to offer Jones out-of-warranty assistance without even looking at her car; nor did they ever bring up the issue of driver abuse in connection with the incident involving getting stuck in snow. Apparently, some GM zone offices were more enlightened and liberal than others in interpreting what constituted abuse of the THM-200 automatic transmission.

What to Do If Your Car's Manufacturer Hits You with Excuse Number 5

If you are accused by an auto manufacturer of abusing your car, there's a good chance somebody at the zone office level is trying to squirm out of giving you something you have coming to you. Unless you have had your car modified in a way forbidden by the warranty, or have used it in racing, or it has been in an accident, the factory will generally find it impossible to prove that you abused it.

So don't let them cloud the issue with this charge. Current warranty law in the United States stipulates that a product must do what it was sold to do; in the case of a car, this means it must provide reasonably reliable transportation under normally encountered conditions. Your brakes shouldn't wear out after 4,000 miles, your clutch shouldn't burn out after 15,000 miles, and the syn-

chronizers in your manual transmission shouldn't fail
after 25,000 miles, under conditions of normal and proper
use. Nevertheless, consumers are often bamboozled into
paying for these items based on the assertion that abuse
caused premature failure.

In fact, a car must be designed to withstand the normal
amount of abuse it will be subjected to by the average
driver. This is how the courts have usually interpreted
the spirit of warranty law. To the consumer's benefit, the
courts have found in many cases that there exists an implied warranty that a car will be fit for its intended purpose, which includes taking a normal degree of abuse.
Auto manufacturers know this very well, and when they
see that you know it too, they'll usually back off from
claiming abuse as a rationale for not helping you.

As a regional service manager with an auto manufacturer, I got involved in an investigation of a vehicle that,
in my opinion, had been the target of arson. All the phys-
ical evidence clearly indicated to me that somebody had
tried to burn the car to a crisp and make it look like an
electrical system fire. When I confronted the car's owner
with the evidence, he was noticeably shaken, and be-
trayed his guilt with his demeanor and some of the in-
criminating comments he made. Despite all this, under
advice of corporate counsel, I paid to have his car fixed
under a special warranty policy after he made it clear to
our home office that he wouldn't relent. Our company
lawyers informed me that regardless of the service division's convictions that the car was torched for insurance
money, we would lose in court. The reason? The courts
are not sympathetic to any allegations on the part of auto
manufacturers that an owner has abused his vehicle, even
when pretty strong proof is available. I guess our lawyers
interpreted arson as merely an extreme case of abuse!

A Basic Strategy for Dealing with the Factory

From the incidents I related pertaining to the THM-200 transmission lawsuit, you can see that there were many inconsistencies in the way General Motors treated its customers. Stingy to some consumers, the company was generous to others. In fact, General Motors *voluntarily* spent tens of millions of dollars trying to help out many car owners whose transmissions had failed. Unfortunately, because of less than admirable treatment of thousands of consumers by some zone offices, GM got sued, and was forced to spend additional millions of dollars.

The Skelton v. General Motors litigation proved extremely costly to GM, but the corporation learned something from it, as did the rest of the auto industry. I don't expect a repetition of the THM-200 debacle soon, because GM is building cars a lot better than it used to. As of this writing, I'd say their cars are as good as or better than any made in America or abroad, and I recommend them as wise choices in terms of quality, comfort and reliability.

But when problems do come up, GM might be expected to be a bit more responsive than it was when confronted with the THM-200 mess. All the major car companies are now pretty shell-shocked from lawsuits. And all of them would like to avoid litigation and the attendant bad publicity. So concerned are the auto manufacturers about lawsuits that lawyers have begun to assume an increasingly more important role in everyday business operations. According to an article appearing in the February 15, 1988 issue of *Automotive News*, a leading auto industry newspaper, lawyers are now involved in product development, manufacturing, and marketing in the car companies where they are employed. Supposedly their legal skills can be utilized to help prevent situations from evolving that might lead to a spate of lawsuits.

How to Negotiate with the Factory

You as a consumer can use this climate of fear of lawsuits to your advantage. Auto manufacturers would prefer to avoid tangling with well-informed consumers. If you present yourself as a knowledgeable person who has insight into how the auto industry operates, the legal eagles at the factory will consider you a high risk in a courtroom confrontation. They would rather give you what you want than fight; in most cases it's cheaper for them.

This doesn't mean that you should preface your requests for out-of-warranty assistance with the threat of litigation. Use a little more finesse than that. What you have to do is subtly touch the litigation nerve at the factory so that they suspect that you *might* be setting them up for a lawsuit. This gives the factory the chance to accommodate you without appearing to have capitulated to you. Remember, the people at the factory have egos, so they don't enjoy losing. If you leave them no choice but to fight, they probably will.

One thing the factory legal experts dread having to fight about is a safety issue. If, in your communications with the factory, you stress that in your opinion the problem with your car has adverse safety implications that could result in an accident and injury, the factory will generally take prompt action. Product liability lawsuits cost auto manufacturers millions of dollars in legal fees and settlement costs. Once you put the factory on notice that a problem exists for which they could be held liable, you can bet that they'll want to stop the trouble before it blows up in their faces.

With this in mind, I recommend that you pursue the following actions if you have trouble with your car out-of-warranty, and feel that the factory should pay for at least part of the cost of correcting it.

1. Gather up all your records that provide evidence that you have maintained your car in accordance with the manufacturer's recommendations.

2. If possible, give a franchised dealership (preferably the one where you bought your car) the first opportunity to address your needs. Discuss your car's problems with your dealer's service manager. If he can't help you, talk to the owner of the dealership. If you strike out there, express your requests in writing to the owner. Some very large dealerships have absentee owners, in which case you should try to contact the general manager (not the sales manager). In either case, be polite. Don't make threats, especially of a lawsuit. If you have purchased more than one car of the kind you are driving, point out your past loyalty to the car line. Indicate that you are seriously considering another purchase, conditional upon a satisfactory resolution of the current difficulty. The dealer may be willing to help you out, either to acquire you or to retain you as a customer. You may not be able to wait to have your car fixed. If it must be repaired quickly, consider having the repairs done by a dealership service department, as this will make it easier to enlist the support of the factory later on.

3. If you strike out with the dealer, send a letter to the factory zone office customer relations department. The address is in your owner's manual. Send them copies of your records that show that you had the same complaint before. If your car's problem is not related to a previous complaint, at least send records that show you have properly maintained your car. State your car's vehicle identification number, its current mileage, date of purchase, and selling dealer. Clearly describe your problem and state what you expect the factory to do for you. Request a personal meeting with the district service manager who represents the factory in your area.

If the problem with your car in any way has safety implications, advise the customer relations department of this in your letter. For example, suppose your car has had a history of hesitation and stalling, for which it was fixed a number of times under warranty. Let the factory know the same trouble has recurred and that you are worried about your safety. After all, what happens if you get stuck in a busy intersection because the engine hesitates unexpectedly? Stress the reasons you believe your car is a potential hazard. Factory customer relations personnel are trained these days to spot potential product liability litigation in the making. You'll probably get some positive action using this approach.

If you have a problem with engine performance and your car's mileage is under 50,000 miles and it is less than 5 years old, you might tell the factory you're concerned about a possible emissions violation. Emission (air pollution) control systems are covered by a separate 5 year/50,000 mile warranty. The factory will generally opt to rectify your car's problem under the emissions warranty than risk your contacting the U.S. Environmental Protection Agency with a complaint. Such a complaint could lead to a formal investigation and stiff fines levied against the manufacturer.

4. If the factory's customer relations department doesn't give you the response you want, or if you fail to get results from a personal meeting with the factory's district service manager, find out if any service bulletins have been issued pertaining to the problem you are having with your car. Also find out if there are any special extended-warranty programs applicable to your car. The procedure for doing this has already been described earlier in this chapter. If you are able to dig up something relevant, notify the customer relations department and the district service manager of your findings. They may reopen your case.

5. If you still can't get satisfaction from the customer relations department or the district service manager, write a certified letter to the factory's general counsel. You can simply address it to the legal department. Once again, explain your position, outline your demands, and inform the addressee that you would like to avoid a lawsuit and wish to have your faith in the product reaffirmed. At this point make it clear that you are aware of your various options, including notifying federal agencies, filing a lawsuit, and so on, but you would prefer a less drastic measure. Drive home the safety issues if they are applicable. Your persistence could be rewarded with at least an offer to give you free parts, while you absorb labor costs to fix your car. Be ready to compromise—writing a few letters isn't too time consuming. Going to court is, and you certainly should try to avoid it whenever possible.

What You Must Avoid Talking About in Your Communications with the Factory

Litigation

A car manufacturer will spend a lot of money to buy customer goodwill, but only when there is a chance the money will be well spent. If you're so incensed that you're obviously threatening a lawsuit, the factory will assume that they have lost you as a future customer, and they won't spend a few bucks to try to make you happy now.

The Better Business Bureau, Consumer Affairs Departments, Government Agencies, Etc.

Don't carbon copy your correspondence to the factory to federal regulatory agencies, consumer groups, and the like. You'll only make it harder for the factory's customer relations department to justify paying you off to shut you up. Once the cat's out of the bag it's too late. Auto manufacturers would prefer to buy their way out of trouble with consumers quietly. Show them that you're a whistleblower and they might dig in their heels and tell you to go take a hike. The bottom line—*negotiate* with people at the factory. Don't start off trying to extort financial help from them.

A Complete Loss of Faith in the Car Line

Even if you think your DreamMobile is a lemon, never tell the factory you think it stinks and would never buy another one. Really now, what kind of diplomacy does that show? If you owned a store, would you be anxious to help a disgruntled customer who prefaces his demands with the stipulation that he never intends to do business with you again?

6

▼ ▼ ▼

Are Independent Repair Shops Better Than Dealer Service Departments?

Studies have shown that only about 20 percent of all car owners continue to have their vehicles serviced by an authorized dealer after expiration of the warranty. For a variety of reasons, motorists generally don't trust dealers to perform good service and opt to do business with independent garages and specialty shops. Aware of this, the National Automobile Dealers Association (NADA) has sounded the alarm to its members, exhorting them to pay more attention to their service departments in order to maintain customer loyalty.

NADA is worried because new car sales are down and costs associated with operating a car dealership are increasing. Consequently, service revenue will play a more important role in ensuring the financial health of franchised dealers. Dealers often don't care too much about keeping their service departments competitive when cars are selling well, because their shops are essentially subsidized by the factory. Up to their necks in factory warranty work that they barely can handle, dealers aren't concerned about how much work the independent shops are getting. But when new-car sales drop, warranty work tapers off, too, so competition for customer-paid repairs becomes important to bolster sagging shop revenue.

Trying to attract a bigger piece of the service pie, dealers will run an assortment of maintenance specials. Suddenly, the absurdly priced $45 oil change and lube job is offered at the more realistic $20 that your neighborhood independent shop has been charging all along. Half-price tune-up bargains are advertised, while the price of the whole menu of maintenance services takes a plunge. But should price be the only factor that you consider in deciding whether to take your car to a dealer or to an independent shop for service? What kind of shop does the best work? And what about the parts they use—will dealers sell you higher-quality parts, the so-called "original equipment"?

Many consumers erroneously believe they will always get better service at an independent shop. Prejudiced against dealers by unpleasant experiences related to past warranty problems, many car owners turn to independent shops, expecting them to be more competent. If you have done this, ask yourself how competently your independent shop could have resolved your warranty complaints. Almost any mechanic can look like a hero doing basic maintenance. Solving warranty problems isn't so easy.

Dealer mechanics get stuck with a lot of nuisance work that's tedious to do. Tracking down rattles in a dashboard, fixing wind noises, water leaks that are sometimes nearly impossible to isolate, miscellaneous suspension clunks and groans, intermittent electrical problems— these are just a few of the tough customer complaints that dealer mechanics have to resolve. And customers can be demanding when it comes to their new cars. Your new car cost you a bundle, so you expect perfection. The dealer's service department gets the brunt of your disappointment when it turns out to be less of a mechanical work of art than you had expected.

So when it comes time to pay for service, all you remember are the rattles and squeaks that couldn't be fixed. Thumbs down to the dealer's service department; you're going to an independent mechanic. But now that you're picking up the tab instead of the factory, the rattles and squeaks that bothered you so much before are tolerable. The love affair with your once shiny new road machine is over. An occasional tune-up, oil change, and brake check will do just fine. If that's all your dealer's mechanics had to do for you, you wouldn't have become disillusioned with them to begin with. When you got your car fixed under warranty, the dealer's mechanics were forced to play by different rules than those which apply to independent mechanics doing customer-paid work. Unless you take these rules into account, you can't make a fair judgment as to which type of facility, dealer or independent, is more competent.

Warranty Work Versus Customer-paid Repairs—Different Rules Apply

When a dealer's mechanic works on your car under warranty, usually he is confronted with a difficult troubleshooting task. Contrast this with the simple routine maintenance generally performed by many independent shops. Routine maintenance merely calls for the replacement of certain parts. Troubleshooting can require many hours of a mechanic's time before he can even determine what has to be replaced. And after he has made this determination, he may not be able to replace the part anyway.

Under warranty, many parts have to be fixed. The factory often will not pay for replacement of complete assemblies. And if the mechanic misdiagnoses the problem, the factory might not pay at all. Things are sometimes a lot easier for an independent mechanic. For example, if you have a rear-wheel-drive car with a rear-axle assembly problem, chances are, an independent mechanic won't fix the rear-axle assembly, something a dealer's mechanic may be required to do. Instead, he will more likely get a good used one from a junkyard or buy a new assembly from a dealer's parts department, and install it in your car. There's much less likelihood of a malfunction in a new or factory rebuilt unit or even a good used one than one that has been repaired.

Because the independent mechanic usually replaces parts instead of fixing them, there's less potential for error and subsequent customer dissatisfaction. The independent mechanic doesn't have to worry about whether a rear-axle assembly's ring-and-pinion gears are bad, or if the pinion bearings or the carrier bearings or the side gears are bad, or if there is too much cross-shaft wear or free play, or too much axle-spline wear, and so on. He just replaces *everything* as an assembly, and voilà, your car is fixed!

Where Do the Best Mechanics Work?

Considering the added difficulty a dealer's mechanic faces doing warranty work compared to customer-paid repairs, you shouldn't let a few bad experiences with warranty service be the only basis for concluding that independent mechanics are better than dealers' mechanics. In fact, often the opposite is true.

A mechanic employed at a new-car dealership has the

advantage of frequent exposure to the same make of automobile day after day. This kind of repetition can force some useful knowledge into even the thickest skull. So even if a dealer's mechanic isn't naturally a talented technician, skills will rub off on him through the frequency of his exposure to a particular make of car.

Dealers' service departments also have the advantage of close association with the factory. This makes the latest technical information easier to obtain. Furthermore, the U.S. auto manufacturers are making significant advancements in the application of computers to solving service problems. Huge databases of diagnostic information are now available on-line at many dealerships.

Recently however, the automotive aftermarket has been making great strides in providing better training and support for independent mechanics. Much of the technical information made available to dealers can now be obtained by independent mechanics by means of CD-ROM systems which store hundreds of thousands of pages of technical information on discs that are similar to audio compact discs.

These computerized information systems permit a mechanic to tell the computer what a car's problem is, after which the computer searches its database for solutions. The computer locates relevant factory technical bulletins on the CD-ROM disc, and prints the bulletins containing the technical solutions to your car's problem. With this information it is much easier for a mechanic to troubleshoot malfunctions in your car. Examples of such systems are the Alldata Automotive Repair Information System 3, the Mitchell On-Demand Repair Information System, and the General Motors Technical Service Information System, Expertec 15. If you find an independent repair shop that has one of these systems, you will probably have a better chance of getting your car repaired quickly at a reasonable cost.

Various parts suppliers and test equipment manufacturers conduct training seminars designed to keep independent mechanics abreast of the latest developments in automotive technology. Whether or not they avail themselves of these educational opportunities is of course another issue, which is why a mechanic's credentials are so important.

What you need to know is how well trained a mechanic is on your make of car and on the particular system in your car that needs repairs. As I pointed out in Chapter 3, ASE certification and factory-training certificates should be scrutinized along with any technical-school diplomas or seminar certificates a mechanic may have. Like any other worker, a mechanic with above-average skills and training usually commands above-average wages and benefits. This is where dealers often have a big advantage over independent shops. Dealers can generally afford to offer the highest wages and best benefits packages. They usually have better-equipped facilities than independent garages, and typically provide better working conditions. So who do you think is going to attract the best mechanics? There are exceptions to this of course. Sometimes a dealer's mechanic will respond to an entrepreneurial calling to open his own shop. He and his partners may be more interested in building a successful business than worrying about benefits and working conditions. You can get some first-rate service from such a shop.

In fairness to independent mechanics it must be said that they have to be exceptionally talented to do their job well. Because they work on virtually every make of car, they are forced to acquire a vast storehouse of knowledge. Also, the really competent independent mechanics have to be excellent diagnosticians. With the cost of parts escalating, it is not always possible to simply replace several parts in an attempt to correct a malfunction. Thorough diagnosis must be performed to isolate the bad part.

If parts were replaced randomly to correct problems, customers would be lost because of exorbitant repair bills. The only solution is technical competence. Many independent mechanics have it; a lot of others don't. Look for training certificates and ASE certification to improve your chances of finding a mechanic who is a good diagnostician.

Who Does the Best-Quality Work?

Consumers often make the mistake of making price the sole consideration in deciding where to get their cars fixed. Scared away by dealers whose service prices seem high, many car owners are lured into independent shops by low-ball advertising tactics and the promise of getting good work done cheaply. While some bargains do exist in automotive service, you should be suspicious of exceptionally low prices—they often accompany shoddy work and the use of second-rate replacement parts.

Some independent shops keep prices down by cutting back on thoroughness, a commonly used ploy where brake work is concerned. I'll go into the technical details in Chapter 7; for now, suffice it to say that there are many shortcuts that independent mechanics can take in doing brake repairs that dealers' mechanics ordinarily would not consider good procedure. The same is true of engine repairs.

Most dealers will refuse to do major repairs on an engine in a car that has been driven more than 80,000 miles. Instead, they would rather sell you a factory rebuilt motor or a new one—and with good reason. First, a factory unit comes with a warranty. If anything goes wrong with it, the dealer can fix it and bill the factory. This protects the dealer and it benefits you, because your engine warranty is good at any dealer having the same franchise. So, if you're traveling across country in a Ford with a Ford-rebuilt engine, any one of thousands of Ford dealers nationwide can correct an engine problem for free under the warranty.

Another rationale for going with the factory engine is that usually it is more completely rebuilt than one that is repaired at an independent garage. The engine block is specially cleaned to prevent cooling problems. Cylinders are rebored to restore maximum compression, power, and control of oil consumption. The crankshaft is machined to restore a perfect fit. These are only a few of the important features of a factory rebuilt engine that you may not get in one that has been repaired.

Consequently, you're more likely to be satisfied with having a factory rebuilt engine installed in your car by a dealer than having your engine repaired by an independent shop. Knowing the potential for problems with a repaired engine that has already seen more than 80,000 miles of original service, dealers wisely choose to avoid the hassles entirely. On the other hand, independent shops are more ready to compromise quality by doing a patch job on a sick engine, a tactic that only comes back to haunt the customer and the shop in the long run.

Another favorite cost-cutting tactic involves the use of low-quality replacement parts. Some of the so-called aftermarket parts used by independent shops are real junk compared to the original equipment items sold by dealers. On the other hand, there are many aftermarket brands that are superior to original equipment. Make sure you ask for the brand name of any part going into your car. Then check with a few auto parts stores to get an opinion about the quality of that brand.

Occasionally, you may be sold a counterfeit part that is packaged to look like a factory original. If a shop offers you a great bargain on a "factory original" part, keep the box and show it to the parts manager at an authorized dealership. The parts manager can tell you if you purchased an inferior counterfeit part. It has been estimated that the volume of business in counterfeit auto parts has approached three billion dollars a year worldwide. With so many inferior quality counterfeits being sold, it is reasonable for you to be skeptical about the quality of the parts installed in your car.

Where Can You Get the Best Service Prices?

Oil Changes

Assuming quality is equal, shop around to get some good deals on maintenance and repairs. You're throwing money down the drain if you pay a car dealer $45 for a lubrication and oil and filter change that can be obtained elsewhere for $20.

Just make sure that you get motor oil with the correct viscosity and API service classification specified by the manufacturer of your car. Be careful with many of the newer General Motors automobiles that require SAE 5W-30 viscosity oil with an "SG" service classification.

Many consumers believe that an oil with a wide viscosity rating, for example, 10W-50, is better than oil having a more limited range, such as 10W-30. This isn't true. The viscosity index expanders used in wide temperature range oils tend to increase sludge formation and can lead to engine problems. For this reason, it is a good idea to stick with the most narrow viscosity range recommended by the manufacturer of your car.

In addition to being careful about the oil that goes into your car, you should exercise care in selecting an oil filter. Make sure you get a name-brand filter. Some of the cheaper aftermarket filters are as low in performance as they are in price.

Another thing you'll have to make sure of is that all of the important fluid levels in your car are checked. Some bargain-priced lube jobs stop at a shot of grease into the front suspension grease fittings if your car has any, without any attention to power-steering fluid, transmission fluid, rear axle, and so on.

For good discount oil changes and lubrication service, check for specials at your dealer's service department. If the price isn't reasonable, go elsewhere. And don't let some slick salesperson con you into believing that your warranty will be voided if you have your maintenance done at an independent shop. Not only is that untrue, but it is also an illegal warranty "tie-in," that is, an attempt to lock you into dealer-performed service and original equipment parts as a condition for continuing your warranty coverage.

Outside the dealer's domain, you can get excellent discount oil changes and lubrication at quick-service specialty shops such as Jiffy Lube, where they throw in a lot of nice additional maintenance services at no extra charge. You'll also get great bargains on oil changes at Goodyear Auto Service Centers, Firestone MasterCare Car Service centers, Sears auto service shops, and a variety of independent garages.

Whatever shop you choose, though, you can tell which one did a thorough job by checking your door hinges and battery. Door hinges should be lubricated periodically and battery terminals should be checked and cleaned at regular intervals. If these items were not attended to, you have good reason to be dissatisfied with the service.

Exhaust System Work

When your car needs a muffler or other exhaust system work, you'll be hard pressed to find any shop that can give you a better deal than Midas, Meineke, or some of the other large discount muffler chains. They're relatively inexpensive, they're extremely fast, and they know what they are doing.

On the other hand, with a few exceptions, I suggest you steer clear of car dealers for exhaust system work. Their volume of this kind of service is low and their prices are generally high. And because of the higher wages they usually pay their mechanics, they can't afford to do exhaust system work competitively.

Tune-Ups

Basic maintenance tune-ups can be among the most overpriced services you can purchase for your car. Most late-model cars don't require tune-ups in the traditional sense (see Chapter 7 for deatils), but many shops still advertise them as though they involved a lot of complex work.

Usually, all that is done is a spark-plug replacement, and an air and fuel filter replacement. The required skills are minimal. Therefore, *unless your car has an engine performance problem,* you can be price conscious as far as tune-ups are concerned. Often, this means choosing an independent shop to do tune-up work instead of a dealer.

This holds true for tune-ups done as a matter of routine maintenance, that is, having the spark plugs and filters changed because your owner's manual says it's time to do it. But when you're having a peculiar starting problem with your car, or when your engine begins to run like it has asthma, you may need the generally superior diagnostic skills available at a dealer's service department. Often, dealers can afford the latest and best test equipment. This includes sophisticated engine and exhaust gas analyzers, without which a mechanic must resort to guessing, and a lot of unnecessary parts replacement, especially on computerized late-model cars.

As an alternative to dealers' service departments, though, there are some excellent diagnostic shops that specialize in untangling the knotty engine performance problems that come up in today's computerized automobiles. Some of them will handle basic tune-up maintenance inexpensively. Just be prepared to pay heavily for troubleshooting time and fault isolation if new spark plugs don't solve your engine's problem. And remember, a top-of-the-line engine analyzer goes for about $30,000, so don't expect a shop to use such a machine on your car for peanuts!

Of the various shops specializing in maintenance tune-ups and more complicated engine-performance diagnosis, some Precision Tune shops are among the best. The parent corporation has been spending an enormous amount of money on technical training assistance for their franchisees. Additionally, Precision Tune shops usually have the most sophisticated test equipment available, *and* a dynamometer. A dynamometer permits the diagnostician to check out a car under a simulated load, as though it actually were being driven on a highway. This can make diagnosis much faster and more accurate than simply revving up an engine with the vehicle standing still in the shop.

Most Precision Tune shops employ a master diagnostician (which Precision Tune calls a "Four Star" technician) who has undergone extensive specialized training in modern automotive electronics and computer systems diagnosis. To verify that the Precision Tune location you are considering employs such a technician, ask to see his Precision Tune training certificate. It is not absolutely necessary that the Four Star technician do the work on your car. Nevertheless, he should be available to other technicians in the shop for consultation. This can ensure faster diagnosis of your car's problems and a lower repair bill.

Brake Jobs

Don't look for bargains in brake work—you could pay for that mistake with your life. The quality of workmanship in brake repairs varies drastically from shop to shop, depending on the knowledge and conscientiousness of the mechanic doing the work. It can also vary depending on the shop's willingness to expose itself to a personal injury and negligence lawsuit if a motorist gets into an accident due to faulty brake repairs.

Dealers generally are not willing to take this risk, so they can be counted on for some pretty competent brake work, but at prices that can be relatively high. I think it's worth it. You can also get predictably good brake repairs at some of the larger franchised service centers operated by tire companies such as Goodyear and Firestone. Many Midas shops also offer very competent brake repairs.

The advent of anti-lock braking systems (ABS) is making the business of brake repair a lot more complex than it used to be. Because ABS systems are computer controlled, brake repair may not be as simple as replacing pads and shoes. For the correction of certain malfunctions, you may find that you have no choice but to return to your dealer for repairs because independent shops may not have the vaguest idea about how to solve the problem.

As a rule of thumb, if you simply want to have your brake linings checked and replaced as a matter of routine maintenance, any competent dealership or independent shop can do the job. However, if an ABS warning light illuminates on the instrument panel, you would be wise to return to an authorized dealership for diagnosis and repair.

Wheel Alignment

There is not much difference between the price of wheel alignments performed by car dealers and those done in specialty shops. But there often can be a big difference in the results.

The ability to do a good wheel alignment depends on having a high-quality alignment machine that is properly calibrated. Car dealers don't do a high volume of alignments, and they often neglect the equipment. On the other hand, tire stores do alignments every day, and they have a stronger interest in keeping their alignment machines in good shape.

They are also concerned about preserving the life of the tires they sell. Customers get pretty angry when their new tires begin to wear out after a few thousand miles of driving. To make sure this doesn't happen, good tire stores take wheel alignments pretty seriously. For them it's a bread-and-butter business. For car dealers it's a sideline. So for wheel alignments, I suggest you stick with tire shops like Goodyear, Firestone, and the like.

Automatic-Transmission Repairs

Transmission specialty shops such as AAMCO and Lee Myles generally do excellent work. I haven't found them to be less expensive than car dealers as far as automatic-transmission work is concerned, but they are usually a lot faster. If you don't want to tie your car up in the shop for a long time, AAMCO or Lee Myles are safe choices.

They keep several "swing units" in inventory. These are transmissions that have already been rebuilt. If they have the right one in stock for your car, you might be in and out of the shop in just a couple of hours. Even if they don't have a swing unit, they keep a large inventory of replacement parts that they can use to fix your transmission quickly. On the other hand, many new-car dealers don't stock a sufficient number of automatic transmission parts, a fact that can lead to annoying and inconvenient delays in getting your car back on the road.

As far as AAMCO is concerned, I have been impressed with the thoroughness of the work turned out by some of their shops. They typically rebuild a transmission much more carefully than a dealer's mechanic would. Not only do they replace clutches and seals, but they also put in new thrust bearings and bushings. That's probably one of the reasons they can offer such a good warranty.

But if you happen to be a die-hard loyalist where your car dealer is concerned, don't overlook the fact that many dealers that take in automatic transmission work sublet the jobs to a specialty shop such as AAMCO or Lee Myles. Even if you have some aversion to these specialty shops, your car might wind up there anyway. But if they're good enough for car dealers to trust, why shouldn't you trust them too?

Manual-Transmission Repairs

Manual, or standard, transmissions can be much more difficult to repair than automatic. Without special tools supplied by the car manufacturer, occasionally they are impossible to fix. The factory forces its dealers to purchase the required tools. But nobody forces independent shops to do so. And since they don't have the volume of manual-transmission repairs to justify it, they generally don't bother to buy the factory tool kits.

There are some pretty good specialty shops that overhaul manual transmissions. However, I've seen numerous long delays getting them fixed at these places because of the lack of special tools. Your best bet? Go to a new car dealer's service department for manual-transmission repairs.

7

▼ ▼ ▼

How to Avoid the Most Costly Auto Repair Rip-offs

Just about every motorist has a favorite horror story to tell about having been ripped off by an auto repair shop. Although you can no more easily prevent auto mechanics from gypping you than you can plumbers, lawyers, or doctors for that matter, there are steps you can take to protect yourself.

Naturally, step one involves finding a good mechanic. In Chapter 6 I offered some suggestions as to what kinds of shops best do certain types of repairs. So, selecting the right shop for your car's problem will help you get the most out of your auto-repair dollar.

But even if you're doing business with a competent repair facility, you should not place yourself completely at their mercy. They're in business to make money. That means they will usually try to sell you whatever it is that is most profitable for them. The only way you can avoid spending money on your car unnecessarily is to have some idea of what kind of service it really needs and how that service should be done most economically.

That's where step two comes in—acquiring some knowledge about how much maintenance your car really needs to keep it safely on the road. And how do you know if a mechanic is over-repairing or under-repairing your car? Can you intelligently decide how repairs should be done to your car without becoming a mechanic yourself?

To answer these questions, let's look at a few of the typical maintenance tasks that will be done on your car and how you can exercise some control over the quality and cost of these services. Keep in mind that the list of maintenance items covered in this chapter is by no means exhaustive. I've deliberately limited the discussion to those tasks that, in my experience, account for the bulk of wasted consumer auto repair dollars.

Oil Changes and Lubrication

Can You Trust a Dealer?

I know a lot of people who don't trust car dealers to do an oil change because they have doubts as to whether or not the old oil will really be drained. Skeptics don't like the idea of being kept out of the shop and not seeing the work done, which often happens at dealers.

I've never seen a dealer's service department deliberately fail to change the oil when paid to do so by a customer, so I don't think the skepticism is warranted. Nevertheless, I can understand why some people have grown suspicious. As a shop manager I've had more than one customer return after an oil change asserting that the oil had not been drained. The basis for the claim? In each case the customer drove the car several miles and later checked the oil, only to find it dark and apparently dirty. To convince a customer that my shop had not engaged in petty larceny, I ordered the oil and filter changed again in the customer's presence. Then, after running the engine a few minutes, we checked the dipstick, and once again, the oil appeared dark and dirty. It's perfectly normal, and if you notice it in your car, don't worry about it.

How Often Should Motor Oil Be Changed?

Except under severe operating conditions, you would be wasting your money having your car's oil changed every 3 months or 3,000 miles as some people suggest. Advocates of this short oil-change interval seem to have trouble adjusting to advances in technology that have made the old rules of good car maintenance obsolete. Motor oil is a lot better than it was 20 years ago and it provides superior lubrication over extended mileage.

Not only is the oil better, but so are the cars, and this further reduces the need for very frequent oil changes. In the days when carburetors reigned supreme, precise fuel mixture control in each cylinder, particularly during cold starts, was extremely difficult. Engine stalling, sputtering, and surging due to excessively lean or rich fuel mixture during warm-up was commonplace. At idle, unequal distribution of fuel in the intake manifold often caused "lean misfiring," a condition in which a cylinder didn't always fire because the fuel mixture was too weak. As a result, contamination of the oil by the occasional presence of too much unburned gasoline in the combustion chamber was almost inevitable. This necessitated frequent oil changes. Another factor that resulted in additional contamination of the motor oil in older cars was their greater tendency toward erratic ignition performance. Equipped with conventional breaker-point ignition systems, these cars were prone to misfire from time to time due to conditions such as breaker-point bounce, distributor-cam wear and dwell variation, inadequate spark coil saturation, and other factors. This is no longer true. Modern cars have much more advanced ignition systems that operate at higher voltages and virtually never misfire unless a defect is present. Further mitigating against contamination of the motor oil is the near-perfect performance of modern multiport fuel-injected engines during cold starts and initial warm-up. With computerized fuel-injection systems providing optimal cold-start enrichment and a running mixture close to the ideal 14.7:1 average air/fuel ratio in each cylinder, the chances of oil contamination by raw gasoline are remote.

Assuming that your car's engine has been running normally with no starting problems and no misfiring, and assuming that you haven't been driving through dust storms, towing a trailer, or doing mostly short-trip stop-and-go driving, you can safely go to the limit of the oil change interval recommended by the car manufacturer.

What About Oil Quality?

Don't assume all motor oil is of suitable quality for your car. Furthermore, don't make the assumption that your mechanic will sell you top-quality oil. If you have any doubts, ask!

Oil quality is indicated on the container by the American Petroleum Institute (API) designation. Most car manufacturers specify an API "SG" quality oil for use in late-model gasoline engines. The letters "SG" indicate that the oil is capable of providing proper engine lubrication under severe service conditions. Even if your owner's manual says that a lower-quality oil ("SF" for example) will suffice, go with the better quality—the price difference is negligible.

Another number found on oil containers indicates the viscosity or thickness of the oil. This is the Society of Automotive Engineers (SAE) grade number, which has nothing to do with oil quality. Typical SAE grade numbers for multigrade oils are 10W-40, 5W-30 and so on. Check your owner's manual and ask your mechanic for the viscosity the manufacturer specifies in consideration of the average outside temperature. Be especially careful with some late-model cars that require SAE 5W-30 motor oil. Many repair shops and service stations don't carry this grade.

If you're going to have your car serviced by a shop that uses bulk oil instead of individual containers, you will have to take their word that the oil they're using has the right API service classification and SAE grade. New-car dealers can usually be trusted to sell you the correct oil for your car because the auto manufacturers send representatives to the dealers to check on this from time to time. But if you're skeptical about oil that comes out of a large storage tank instead of a quart can, you might have to go elsewhere for oil changes. In either case, don't waste your money on an oil change that doesn't include a new filter.

Are All Oil Filters the Same?

There's a wide range in the quality of oil filters available. Genuine factory parts supplied by car dealers are all pretty good, so you can count on getting a good oil filter at a dealership's service department. Aftermarket oil filters can be much better than original equipment or a lot worse. Inferior quality filters won't trap the tiny particles that slowly eat away at an engine. Make sure you are getting a name brand to be on the safe side.

What About Oil Additives?

Beware of low-priced oil-change bargains that go up in cost with the addition of useless additives. Unless your car's engine is on its last laps around the track and burning oil and knocking ferociously, most oil additives will do no good. An old clunker may quiet down and burn less oil for a while as a result of pouring an oil thickener in the crankcase. But good-quality motor oil already contains all the additives a normal engine needs.

Special Caution for Cars with Turbochargers

If you own a car equipped with a turbocharger, getting the oil changed is not as simple as it is for nonturbocharged cars. Turbochargers run at very high speeds and require adequate lubrication at all times. If a turbocharger operates without lubrication for even a short time it can be damaged.

Damage can occur after an oil change if the engine is started without first priming the turbocharger. During the brief time it takes for the engine's oil passages to fill, the turbocharger will have achieved very high speed. Starved for oil for this short period, the turbocharger can experience severe bearing damage.

To avoid this, the engine must be cranked *without starting* for as long as it takes for the oil pressure warning light to go out. After the engine has been primed, it can be started without damaging the turbocharger. Unfortunately, many shops forget to take this precaution. If your car is turbocharged, be certain to remind your mechanic to prime the oil passages before starting the engine.

What Is a Good Lubrication?

Most advertised oil changes include a lubrication. Most cars never get the lubrication as advertised.

More often than not mechanics don't bother to "check all fluid levels" as they should. Remind the shop manager that you want power-steering fluid and automatic-transmission fluid checked and topped up as needed. If you have a rear-wheel drive car, the rear-axle lubricant should be checked and topped up as well. Brake fluid, coolant, and windshield-washer solvent should also be checked.

Of course, a lubrication should also include pumping some chassis grease into suspension and steering-linkage grease fittings. Beyond this customary service, however, attention should be paid to door and trunk hinges and latches, shift linkages, and parking-brake cables. It only takes a couple of minutes to lubricate these items, but they are rarely tended to. If you make the mistake of letting your mechanic get away with this oversight, you could wind up paying for an expensive repair that could have been easily prevented with a little oil or grease.

Tune-Ups

Engine tune-ups often are grossly overpriced. If you own a car built in the late 1980s, it only requires a simple periodic *maintenance tune-up*, so you would be wasting your money paying for the old-fashioned "complete tune-up." But a lot of consumers are suckered into doing just that anyway because old auto-service habits die hard.

Not long ago many automobile engines required complete tune-ups as often as every 6,000 miles. Few cars could be driven more than 12,000 miles without a noticeable deterioration in performance. Consequently, motorists got conditioned to the idea of an annual engine tune-up, that is, new points, spark plugs, condenser, ignition-timing adjustment, new fuel and air filters, carburetor adjustment, and perhaps replacement of the distributor cap and rotor. The one part of the car most responsible for the need for routine tune-up service was the distributor, and particularly, the breaker points and condenser (Figure 1) mounted inside it. New technology has changed this.

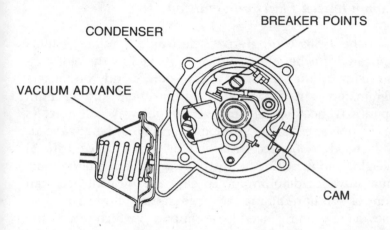

Figure 1. The breaker points found in old-fashioned ignition distributors required frequent replacement. The cam also had to be lubricated periodically to prevent premature failure of the breaker points. New technology has eliminated these maintenance headaches. Modern distributors do not use breaker points.

Transistorized Ignition

In the 1970s ignition points and condensers went the way of the dinosaur as these primitive ignition parts gave way to breakerless transistorized ignition systems. The miracle of space-age solid-state electronics was beginning to make its impact in the automobile industry. But old habits died hard as mechanics who had been accustomed to installing new points and condensers instead unnecessarily replaced distributor-pulse generators. These electromagnetic ignition parts did not function in any way like points and condensers, but since they were located in approximately the same position in the distributor, many mechanics mistakenly replaced them anyway, even though no routine service was actually required.

Computerized Electronic Ignition

In the 1980s computerized electronic ignition systems appeared, further altering the role played by the old-fashioned distributor. Not only were points and condensers eliminated, but the traditional centrifugal and vacuum spark advance mechanisms were done away with too. As an engine speeds up, ignition timing must be advanced. This used to be accomplished by a set of centrifugal weights mounted in the distributor and an external vacuum advance diaphragm. These mechanical devices can control ignition timing advance rather imprecisely, so they have been replaced by a computer, which can do the job with incredible precision. And unlike centrifugal weights and vacuum advance devices, computers don't need periodic maintenance. Moreover, thanks to the computer, it is generally not necessary to ever adjust basic ignition timing. One less thing for a mechanic to do!

Computerized "Distributorless" Ignition

The next step in the evolution of automotive ignition systems involved getting rid of distributors entirely. In the two systems previously described, a rotating "rotor" distributes high-voltage (supplied by a spark coil) to the spark plug at each cylinder via a distributor cap and ignition wires (Figure 2). The distributor can wear out. The distributor cap and rotor require periodic replacement because they burn out. In modern "distributorless" ignition systems the distribution of electrical energy to the spark

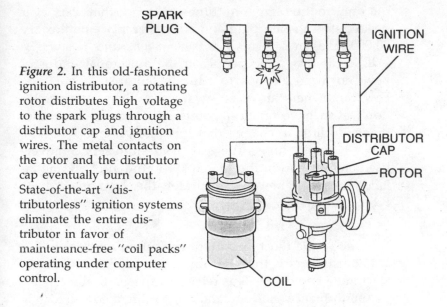

Figure 2. In this old-fashioned ignition distributor, a rotating rotor distributes high voltage to the spark plugs through a distributor cap and ignition wires. The metal contacts on the rotor and the distributor cap eventually burn out. State-of-the-art "distributorless" ignition systems eliminate the entire distributor in favor of maintenance-free "coil packs" operating under computer control.

plugs is handled by a coil pack and an electronic control unit, which is really a computer. The entire distributor is eliminated, and with it, the need to service the cap and rotor.

So What's Left to Tune?

One of the major benefits offered by computerized electronic ignition and distributorless ignition is the elimination of annual tune-ups. Many cars built since 1981 simply cannot be "tuned" in the traditional sense. In fact, a label located in the engine compartment on these cars clearly advises that no tune-up service is required. The same information is contained in the owner's manuals.

Yet, few consumers read owner's manuals and fewer read the tune-up specifications labels in their vehicles' engine compartment. If they did, they would find out that the only routine ignition "tune-up" work their cars ever needed was a spark plug and air filter replacement every 30,000 miles or so. This is a basic *maintenance tune-up.*

It seems that some people in the auto-repair industry have not been anxious to educate motorists about this. Few car owners are even aware that their automobiles don't even have ignition points, yet tune-up advertisements do little to change that misconception.

For example, here's the text of an auto-service advertisement that ran in the March 1988 edition of a Long Island suburban newspaper under the banner "Advice From the Expert:"

One of the most important and often overlooked adjustments is the one-way relationship between timing and dwell. This relationship is critical if top performance, mileage and engine life are desired. Unfortunately, many mechanics and weekend knucklebusters aren't even aware such a relationship exists. When setting either timing or dwell (adjusting the distributor points), remember that when you change the dwell you also change the timing. If you set the timing, however, the dwell doesn't change. Always set the dwell angle first, then set the timing. This is often confusing and always illogical; but that's the way it is.

Fifteen years ago the copy in this ad would have been pretty informative to the consumer. However, considering that since the early 1970s almost no cars have been manufactured with ignition points, the relationship between timing and dwell is irrelevant. However, because a lot of mechanically naïve motorists still think their cars need conventional tune-ups, this kind of advertising could sound technically impressive enough to attract customers. Unless you're driving an antique, save your money—*annual* complete tune-ups are lucrative for mechanics but won't do your car any good.

If you make the mistake of paying for an *annual* tune-up on a computer-controlled fuel-injected engine, you're just spending a lot of money for some new spark plugs and a couple of new filters. This is all that a basic *maintenance tune-up* entails. There is no carburetor to adjust, and fuel-injection systems are largely nonadjustable. Therefore, instead of an annual tune-up, all you really need is a basic *maintenance tune-up* which should be done according to the schedule in your owner's manual, usually every 30,000 miles, not annually.

Read the fine print on a lot of tune-up advertisements and you'll notice they say "replace spark plugs, check all wires, check all emission hoses, check timing, check this, check that; check . . ., check . . ., check." Lots of checks but no real work. Unless there's something abnormal about the way the car runs after a basic maintenance tune-up, none of the so-called checks are likely to be done.

This doesn't mean, however, that your car will not require periodic ignition-system or fuel-system work. If your car does not run properly, a basic maintenance tune-up probably will not correct the problem. In this situation your car needs specialized diagnosis of the computerized *engine management systems* using sophisticated test equipment. Unfortunately, many shops still mistakenly call this kind of work tune-up service, even though it involves much more than a tune-up and costs a lot more.

As a rule, you should not pay for a basic maintenance tune-up unless your car calls for one according to the maintenance schedule in the owner's manual. If your car is not running properly and it is not scheduled for a maintenance tune-up, ask for diagnosis of the engine management systems. This kind of service costs much more than a tune-up, but you'll save the money you would have spent for unnecessary tune-up work.

A complete engine diagnosis can reveal a variety of problems responsible for a poorly running engine. One of the more difficult-to-diagnose problems that has been turning up in many late-model cars is heavy carbon buildup on the engine's intake valves, in the intake manifold, and in the idle air control motors of many fuel-injected cars. This will be discussed later on in this chapter.

What About Carburetor Adjustments?

Very few cars built these days are equipped with carburetors. Those that are, do not require fuel-mixture adjustments. In fact, modern carburetors are designed in such a way that the mixture can't be adjusted even if a mechanic wanted to. About all that can normally be tinkered with is idle speed.

By the early 1990s, virtually every car made will have fuel injection instead of a carburetor. Fuel-injection systems are controlled by an on-board computer which regulates idle speed, air/fuel mixture, and total fuel quantity delivered to each cylinder. The computer runs the whole show, so adjustments generally are not possible.

How Much Should a "Tune-Up" Cost?

To avoid wasting a lot of money on unnecessary annual tune-ups, first check your owner's manual to see what kind of tuning your car requires. If you don't have the manual, look for the vehicle emission control information sticker in the engine compartment. If you have a fuel-injected car built since the late 1980s, chances are the sticker will say that no idle mixture, idle speed, or ignition-timing adjustments are possible. There goes your annual tune-up!

Basically, such a car will just need periodic replacement of the spark plugs, fuel filter, and air filter. This is a *maintenance tune-up*. Get these items replaced at the time intervals specified by the manufacturer. On most cars the labor required should not exceed 30 minutes. So, if you have a four-cylinder car, figure about eight to ten dollars for new spark plugs, plus the cost of the filters and 30 minutes worth of labor. If your mechanic tries to charge you for more labor time than that, make him justify it.

Will a "Tune-Up" Fix Your Car If It Doesn't Run Right?

New spark plugs and filters will fill the bill for routine maintenance. But if your car's engine runs like it has the flu, replacing these items will rarely cure the coughing and sputtering. Under these circumstances you are better off trying only a new set of spark plugs, unless they have been replaced recently. If that doesn't work, a complete engine diagnosis is necessary, in which case you are in for some expensive work.

The best computerized engine analyzers cost over $30,000 and require a good technician to exploit their capabilities. However, the results are well worth the bill you'll get for diagnostic time. These machines can analyze ignition systems, computer controls, fuel-injection performance, and even the mechanical condition of the engine. One of the most powerful testers of this type, the MCA Computer Analyzer, is manufactured by Sun Electric Corporation for use in automotive-service facilities. This device is outfitted with a computer of its own to check the computer in your car, as well as other systems in the vehicle. If you find a shop that has one and knows how to use it, you should be able to get your engine performance problems solved quickly without a lot of guesswork common in many shops.

What About Fuel-Injector Cleaning and Gas Additives?

Some tune-up shops advertise fuel-injector cleaning. Fuel-injector cleaning generally is not necessary. In the mid 1980s clogging of electronic fuel injectors became a big problem on cars equipped with so-called multiport fuel-injection systems. Systems of this type have an individual injector (Figure 3) to supply fuel to each cylinder in the engine. On some cars, the part of the injector known as the pintle can accumulate deposits that restrict the flow of fuel out of the injector. This causes rough idle in less severe cases, and engine misfire and poor gas mileage in extreme cases.

Chemists in the petroleum industry went to work on the problem and quickly came up with a solution in the form of special gasoline additives that could actually clean the injectors with the engine operating in normal use. These additives are now found in all good-quality gasolines. Yes, the commercials you have heard on television are true. You really can drive your car's fuel injectors clean!

As I'll explain in the next section, certain gasolines actually have been responsible for causing fuel-injector clogging. If you have been operating your car on a brand of gasoline that is conducive to injector clogging, your engine may run so poorly that it could take several tanks of a good grade of fuel to correct the problem. In this case, fuel-injection cleaning is a reasonable choice, assuming injector obstruction is really the problem. A good diagnostician can locate a clogged fuel injector using sophisticated engine analyzers.

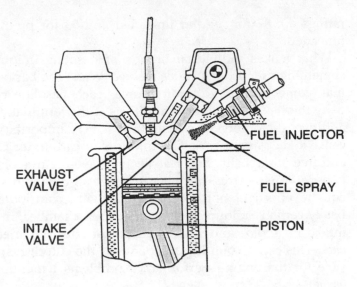

Figure 3. Engines equipped with multiport fuel injection have an individual injector for each cylinder. The fuel spray pattern from the injector must be correct to ensure good engine performance. A dirty injector can leak fuel or produce the wrong spray pattern. Special detergents are added to gasoline to clean fuel injector deposits. Extra additives should not be necessary.

Bad Gasoline and the Engine Carbon Problem

Rough idle, hard starting, stumbling and hesitation, loss of power, and fuel economy—all of these problems can be caused by the gasoline you have been using and may not be related to fuel-injector clogging. Contrary to what you may have heard about all gasolines being the same because they come from the "same pipe," there are big differences among gasoline brands that go beyond octane rating. A gasoline's octane rating, which is posted at the pump, tells you about the fuel's ability to resist *pinging*, an abnormal form of combustion that results in metallic sounding noises inside the engine. Typical octane ratings are 87 for regular unleaded and 93 for premium unleaded.

What makes individual brands of gasoline unique is something called the *additive package*. While the basic fuel may come from a common source, each gasoline company injects its own special additives at the terminal. One additive, the detergent concentrate, is very important because it keeps your car's fuel injectors or carburetor clean and free of deposits, and *may* keep the engine free of carbon deposits. I stress *may* because not all detergents are equally effective, and some can actually contribute to heavy carbon buildup in the combustion chamber, in the intake manifold, and in idle air motors on fuel-injected cars. This carbon buildup frequently is the culprit responsible for the engine performance problems I mentioned earlier.

All gasolines in the past have contained *carburetor detergents*, which did what their name implied—they kept carburetors free of excess deposits. Recently, most cars have been manufactured with fuel-injection systems instead of carburetors. The type of fuel-injection system known as *port fuel injection* was, in the past, prone to injector clogging due to the chemical nature of gasoline. To keep this type of injector from clogging, gasoline companies (at the request of certain auto manufacturers) increased the concentration of carburetor detergent. This alleviated the injector clogging problem, but in many cars, it created an entirely new problem.

At high temperatures, carburetor detergents can be unstable and can cause heavy carbon deposits to build up on the intake valves and in the intake manifolds of many engines. The carbon deposits can interfere with fuel-air flow and the combustion process in the engine, causing a variety of performance problems.

Certain types of engines are more susceptible to these deposit-induced performance difficulties; among them are some engines found in BMWs, Audis, and Volkswagens. These manufacturers design for exceptionally high performance from a small displacement combustion chamber using the so-called *fast burn* technique. Nevertheless, all engines made by every manufacturer can be adversely affected by these carbon deposits. The carbon build-up on the intake valves interferes with a process referred to as combustion chamber *swirl*, thereby slowing combustion and effectively retarding ignition.

To combat intake valve carbon, many gasoline companies have changed their additive packages, substituting *deposit control* additives for carburetor detergents. These chemicals not only keep injectors clean, but they also keep intake valves relatively free of carbon. Gasolines that do the best job of keeping an engine clean meet or exceed the so-called BMW detergency standard.

Unfortunately, if your car manifests symptoms of *heavy* intake valve or intake manifold carbon buildup, deposit control additives will not correct the problem. These chemicals can *prevent* the problem, but cannot correct it entirely once it is present. If rough idle, hard starting, stumbling and hesitation, loss of power, and fuel economy are traced to heavy intake-valve carbon buildup or carbon buildup elsewhere in the induction system of the engine, engine repairs are required. Since increased exhaust emissions have been associated with heavy intake-valve carbon, you should make every effort to have this problem repaired free of charge under your car's five-year/50,000-mile emission-control systems warranty.

Some consumers have met with resistance from dealers to the idea of decarbonizing their engine valves free of charge. In response to complaints about poor engine performance, these dealers have offered to sell the consumer an expensive fuel additive.

These additives are of little use in removing the carbon from an already heavily carbonized engine. As a *preventive* treatment they work fine, but they are unnecessary for regular use now that many gasolines are available that meet the BMW detergency standard, that is, they have deposit-control additives already blended in. Unfortunately, as I previously stated, these gasolines cannot clean an already heavily carbonized engine. Furthermore, many gasolines that are advertised as meeting the BMW standard only meet the standard in certain regions of the country and may fail to comply in other geographical areas.

So, what are your options if you are stuck with a poorly running car and carbon buildup is the culprit? There are two solutions. One is an expensive mechanical procedure for removing carbon. It involves disassembling certain engine parts and blasting the carbon with, of all things, ground nutshells! In the auto-repair business they refer to this treatment as the "walnut." It isn't cheap! The bill just might drive you nuts!

There is, however, a new low-cost chemical treatment that should hold some promise for motorists whose cars are plagued by heavy carbon buildup. Precision Tune Corporation has been working on a procedure to decarbonize engine valves, intake manifolds, and other induction components using a proprietary chemical process. The technique will remove carbon that characteristically builds up in engines equipped with port (multipoint) fuel injection. Available in many Precision Tune shops, this procedure can save car owners a bundle of money. An extraordinarily powerful solvent is introduced into the engine, followed by a chemical neutralizer. Engine oil should be changed after the procedure has been completed. The treatment is reported to be completely safe for engines and will not cause damage to catalytic converters. This appears to be an excellent alternative to the mechanical procedure that physically removes carbon using ground nutshells.

In either case, you probably will meet with little success trying to get your dealer to pay for the repair under warranty. Frequently, dealers allege that the consumer used an improper grade of gasoline. This position seems arbitrary and unrealistic. Cars should be designed to run on the commonly available gasolines. It is doubtful that most consumers would knowingly buy a car that would develop engine trouble as a result of using major brands of fuel. The high concentration of carburetor detergents in gasoline (which produces excessive carbon on intake valves) was blended into the fuel by the gasoline companies at the request of certain car makers. The intention was good—to keep fuel injectors clean. But the creation of an intake-valve carbon problem was not anticipated. Should consumers be made to pay for this miscalculation? I think not. While many gasolines now contain additives that can minimize this problem, there are thousands of motorists whose engines have already incurred serious carbon damage. I think all car manufacturers should assume responsibility for intake-valve decarbonizing up to a reasonable mileage beyond the normal warranty for those motorists who did not have access to the gasolines that now contain the proper additives, or who were not specifically told what fuels to use.

There is an exception that must be addressed however. Not all induction system carbon buildup is due to lack of adequate fuel detergency. Fuel additives can keep intake valves clean but they cannot keep an intake manifold, idle air bypass valve, and certain other parts clean on engines equipped with port (multipoint) fuel injection. On these engines periodic decarbonization is a worthwhile maintenance item for which the car owner is responsible. The carbon buildup in these engines is due in part to the presence in the intake manifold of oil and fuel vapors drawn in by the positive crankcase ventilation system. Gasoline with the right deposit control additives will keep the intake valves clean but will not have any effect on the manifold, etc. This is where Precision Tune's chemical cleaning process can really help because it removes carbon from the intake valves *and* the rest of the induction system.

If you are faced with the cost of decarbonizing your engine's intake valves, I suggest you appeal to the management of your dealership for assistance, and, if that fails, to the carmaker's zone office. As a last resort, you might try contacting the Environmental Protection Agency to inquire about possible assistance under the terms of the vehicle's emissions warranty. This will be discussed more in the next section.

Some motorists might conclude that all the red tape and hassles are not worth the trouble considering that Precision Tune has an inexpensive procedure that may solve the problem. If you would prefer to avoid conflict and don't mind the expense, paying the small price for the repair at Precision Tune might be a reasonable choice. If you would rather stick to your guns and force the issue, the next section outlines an approach that can work.

Don't Pay for Emission Warranty Work!

If you're like most car owners, there's a good chance that you have paid for, or will eventually wind up paying for, repair parts and labor that you could have obtained free.

Many motorists who have been unnecessarily charged for engine tune-ups, PCV valves, new carburetors, fuel injectors, ignition wires, and dozens of other items that should have been taken care of free of charge under the terms of the five-year/50,000-mile vehicle emission controls *design and defect warranty* mandated by the Federal Clean Air Act. Every car and light truck sold in America has this warranty, regardless of whether the vehicle was bought new or used.

Here's a tip that can save you several hundred dollars over the life of your car. If your car's engine is not running correctly, and the vehicle is less than five years old and has been driven less than 50,000 miles, there's a good chance you can get the problem fixed for nothing! Just about anything that can go wrong with a late-model car that adversely affects engine performance generally will be attributable to a problem in one or more items covered under the emission controls warranty.

Unfortunately, most drivers are accustomed to getting an annual engine tune-up because cars used to require regular tuning. It is assumed that a tune-up is the solution to an engine performance problem on a late-model car. As I mentioned previously, a basic *maintenance tune-up* will not correct most engine performance problems.

On many cars, the spark plugs can be used for 30,000 miles, and, therefore, certainly don't need annual replacement. Check your owner's manual for the suggested replacement interval on your car. The spark plugs are covered as emission-control items up to the first suggested replacement interval. So if your car calls for a 30,000-mile spark plug replacement, the plugs are warranted as emission-control items for at least the first 30,000 miles.

In many states, motor vehicle exhaust emissions are tested periodically. If your car fails such a test, you may be entitled to free repairs under the terms of the two-year/24,000-mile emissions *performance warranty*. This warranty supplements the five-year/50,000-mile *design and defect* warranty.

Basically, it provides special provisions in those areas where the state or local government has implemented an emissions *inspection/maintenance* program conforming to Federal guidelines. If your car fails an emissions test and you are required by state or local law to fix it, the manufacturer must absorb the entire cost for the first two years or 24,000 miles, with somewhat more limited liability for five years or 50,000 miles. However, repairs not covered under the *performance warranty* may still be covered under the *design and defect warranty*.

Most consumers are surprised at the large number of under-the-hood components that are covered by the emissions warranty. Here are a few of them:

- Oxygen sensor
- Dual-walled exhaust pipe
- Catalytic converter
- PCV valve
- Fuel injectors
- Carburetor
- On-board computer
- Turbocharger
- Intake manifold
- Exhaust manifold
- Distributor
- Ignition wires
- Spark plugs

Once again, this is only a partial list of covered parts. Unfortunately, it is not always easy to get these items replaced under the emissions warranty. Unwary consumers frequently are charged for these parts by both independent repair shops and franchised car dealers.

Independent repair shops do not have the authority to bill auto manufacturers for warranty work. Consequently, if such a shop discovers an emissions-related defect, they may not apprise you of your option to go to a car dealership where the problem can be corrected free under the emissions warranty. If you select that option, an independent shop legitimately can charge you for diagnostic time, but car dealerships are not permitted to do so as far as the Environmental Protection Agency is concerned. *No charges for diagnostic time are allowed in connection with work required under the emissions warranty.*

Although new car dealers can get reimbursed by the auto manufacturers for emissions warranty work, the amount the manufacturers are willing to pay is often substantially less than the dealer normally charges for nonwarranty work. Consequently, there is an obvious incentive for the dealer to attempt to make you pay for emissions warranty work. Your knowledge of your rights under the warranty and your persistence in demanding fair treatment are your best defenses from inappropriate charges for emissions warranty work.

Both emissions warranties are described in detail in two brochures printed by the U.S. Environmental Protection Agency. One is entitled *What You Should Know About Your Auto Emissions Warranty,* and the other is called *If Your Car Just Failed An Emission Test You May Be Entitled To Free Repairs.* To obtain them call (202) 382–2640 or write to: Warranty Complaint, Field Operations and Support Division, U.S. Environmental Protection Agency, Washington, DC 20460. You can also contact the Field Operations and Support Division to register a complaint if you think your mechanic has charged you for repairs that should have been done under the emission controls warranty. However, before you do this, try to resolve the problem with the management of the car dealership first; if that doesn't work, contact the auto manufacturer's zone office and give them an opportunity to intercede on your behalf.

Brake Repairs

The cost of automotive brake work spans a pretty big price range. At the low end you have discount service centers that frequently advertise bargain-priced brake jobs. At the high end are the new car dealerships that generally show no interest in merchandising brake work at a discount. You should be skeptical of any brake work performed at cut-rate prices. Automotive brake service is one area where few real bargains exist. If the price is exceptionally low, the work is usually second rate. Second-rate brake work can save you a few bucks but could cost you your life.

Disc Brake Rip-offs

Most late-model cars are equipped with front disc brakes and drum brakes on the rear wheels. Many bargain-priced brake jobs amount to no more than a replacement of the disc brake pads. This may not be enough to ensure your safety. In some cases, consumers are baited into a shop by the promise of an inexpensive brake job, only to be sold additional unnecessary work, usually in the form of disc machining. More common, however, are situations where too little, not too much, work is done. In this sense, you are ripped off because you leave the shop with a small bill and a false sense of security about the condition of your car's brakes. Slipshod work at any price is no bargain. Here are a few things a second-rate disc brake job might omit, leading to the possibility of subsequent brake failure and an accident:

- Replacement of cracked flexible brake hoses

- Replacement of crazed discs

- Replacement of discs machined below manufacturer's tolerances

- Draining the brake fluid and flushing the hydraulic brake lines

- Cleaning of sliding caliper support brackets

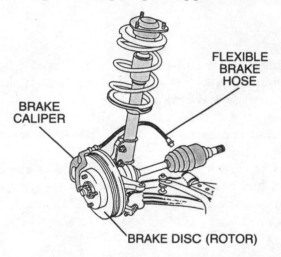

Figure 4. Flexible brake hoses should be inspected for cracks periodically. These hoses must withstand extremely high pressure. Although superficial cracks themselves will not cause leaks, they expose the interior of the hose to damage by road debris.

▶ The Brake Hoses

The flexible hoses (Figure 4) installed on the front brakes must be inspected for damage such as cracks, abrasion, etc. Mechanics frequently forget to do this, especially when performing discount brake jobs. These hoses must handle brake-fluid pressure as high as 1,500 pounds per square inch, so they have to be in good shape. Make sure they are inspected and get the results of the inspection in writing on the repair order.

If your car has more than 80,000 miles on it, it's a good idea to have both front brake hoses replaced even though they show no apparent signs of deterioration. It's cheaper to have this done concurrent with other brake work. So, if you're thinking of getting a discount brake job on a car with a lot of miles on the odometer, be prepared to spring for some extra bucks for new brake hoses.

► *The Brake Discs*

Disc Crazing. A brake disc is said to be crazed when it has small hairline cracks (Figure 5) in the friction surface on which the pads make contact. These cracks are caused by expansion and contraction due to heat. This cycle of expansion and contraction leads to stresses in the disc, metal fatigue, and cracking.

If the cracks are very slight, machining the disc will get rid of them; however, they will probably reappear. Given enough time, what begins as minor crazing will end in severe cracks, disc fracturing, and an accident.

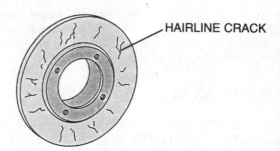

HAIRLINE CRACK

Figure 5. A brake disc (rotor) is said to be "crazed" when it has hairline cracks in its surface. It is not a good idea to machine a crazed disc to get rid of cracks. They will probably recur, causing a serious fracture and the possibility of an accident.

Many mechanics fail to recognize crazing in its early stages, or if they do, they often just machine the discs to clean up the friction surfaces. Saving a customer the cost of new discs might preserve a shop's image as a low-priced service center, but it is not in the customer's best interests.

Disc Machining to Correct Vibration Or Noise. Disc machining, cutting the discs on a lathe, is an area of automotive service where you as a customer are very likely to fall victim to deceit or incompetence because:

► Your car's brake discs really don't require cutting, or

► The discs actually do need to be cut but the job isn't done, or

► The discs are cut dangerously too thin

Several things can go wrong with brake discs that can require machining to restore the friction surfaces. If you feel a pulsation or vibration in the brake pedal or steering wheel when the brakes are applied, it is possible that one or both discs are warped. Technically, "warping" involves problems in a disc's lateral runout or surface parallelism, conditions that can be verified by taking measurements with a dial indicator and a micrometer. Lateral runout refers to a side-to-side wobbling of the disc as it rotates. Lack of parallelism refers to unequal thickness of the disc around its circumference. Both defects are corrected by cutting the disc on a lathe or using an on-car grinder. Another problem which is correctable by cutting the discs on a lathe is surface scoring. Scoring (Figure 6) involves the presence of deep circular grooves in the friction surfaces.

How You Can Tell That Your Car's Discs Need Cutting. Consumers are occasionally conned into paying for disc

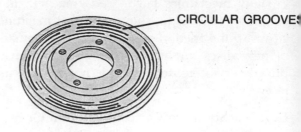

Figure 6. A brake disc (rotor) is said to be "scored" when it has circular grooves worn into its friction surface. If the scoring is not severe, it may not be necessary to machine the disc.

machining that is not necessary to correct a vibration complaint. Sometimes the front discs require machining; not the rear discs or drums. Vibration or pulsation which occurs when you step on the brake pedal is usually caused by "warped" discs or drums. Most cars have disc brakes in the front and drum brakes in the rear. You can tell whether the problem is due to the front discs, the rear drums, or rear discs (if so equipped) fairly easily.

If you feel a severe vibration throughout the car when the brakes are applied forcefully, but the steering wheel itself does not vibrate or shimmy in any way, the problem is most likely due to one or more warped rear drums or rear discs. A warped drum is out-of-round. The only way to correct the problem is by machining both rear drums or discs, or replacing them if their condition does not permit machining. It is never acceptable to machine or replace a drum or disc on one side of the car without machining or replacing the opposite drum or disc. If one drum or disc is replaced, the other should be replaced too to maintain a matched set having equal friction characteristics.

If you feel a slight pulsation in the brake pedal when the brakes are applied gently, the problem is most likely caused by one or both rear drums being slightly out-of-round, or by one or both rear discs being warped. Machining both rear drums or discs and installing new brake shoes will usually correct the condition. On cars equipped with antilock brake systems (ABS), a slight pulsation in the brake pedal during very hard braking is normal. This pulsation is not caused by out-of-round brake drums or warped discs. Instead, it results from the action of the ABS system, whereby the ABS computer causes rapid automatic application and release of the brakes to prevent wheel lockup.

Regarding the aforementioned condition where there is a slight pulsation when the brakes are applied gently, it is entirely possible for the problem to be due to warped front discs and not out-of-round rear drums or warped rear discs. Some front wheel drive cars have a suspension design that can greatly dampen disc brake-related vibrations and isolate these vibrations from the steering wheel. The pulsation could feel like out-of-round rear drums or warped rear discs even though it actually originates at the front discs. There is a simple way to differentiate front disc-related pulsation from rear drum- or rear disc-related pulsation, but great caution must be exercised while performing the test. Here's how it's done.

While driving at about 10 mph on a road where there is no traffic or in a vacant parking lot, take your foot off the gas pedal and gradually apply the parking brake (do not apply the regular brakes). Don't apply the parking brake too forcefully or the rear wheels will lock. If you feel pulsation as the car slows down, the rear drums are out-of-round (or the rear discs are warped if the car is equipped with 4-wheel disc brakes). If there is no pulsation, the problem is in the front discs. After completing the test, make sure you release the parking brake.

If the steering wheel vibrates when you apply the brakes, it is usually due to one or more warped front discs. In the case of discs, warping can mean a side-to-side wobbling of the disc or waviness in the disc's sur-

face. These conditions are corrected by machining both
front discs or replacing them. It is never acceptable to machine or replace a disc on one side of the car without machining or replacing the opposite disc. If one disc is
replaced, the other should also be replaced to maintain a
matched set having equal friction characteristics.

Sometimes (but rarely) vibration can be felt in the steering wheel when the brakes are applied because there is a
problem in the vehicle's front suspension. Badly worn
tie-rod ends or other parts can cause such vibrations.
If normal brake repairs fail to correct a vibration when
the brakes are used, you should have the suspension
checked.

Occasionally, a brake vibration is corrected by machining the discs, shortly after which the vibration comes
back. In some cases the problem is caused by a condition
referred to as "excessive runout" (side-to-side wobbling)
of the wheel hub. The wheel hub is the part the disc is
attached to. The only way to correct this problem is to
replace the hub.

Scoring can also necessitate machining brake discs. To
confirm that your car's discs are scored, you'll have to be
present in the repair shop when the wheels are removed.
Make sure the disc isn't hot when you perform the following check. Run your fingernail across the friction surface of the disc, starting at the disc's inside diameter and
proceeding in a straight line toward the outside diameter.
If you feel grooves with your nail, the disc is scored. If
the disc is smooth, and doesn't have dark blue spots on it
indicating overheating, nothing will be gained by machining it. A mechanic looking to make a few extra bucks off
you might try to sell you some line of baloney about why
machining is needed to restore correct porosity of the cast
iron and the disc's coefficient of friction. There's a kernel
of truth to this, but the results are not worth the cost
when only a new set of replacement pads would work

just fine, assuming other brake system components are okay.

If a disc is scored, it is a good idea to cut it to restore a smooth friction surface. If one front disc is machined, the other must be machined too regardless of whether or not it is also scored. Failure to machine both discs can result in uneven braking. Uneven braking can also result if both discs are not machined to approximately the same final thickness.

If minor disc scoring is present, cutting is not mandatory. However, it will take some time for new brake pads to bed into the grooved discs, and a lot of squeaking and other annoying noises can be expected in the process, along with accelerated initial pad wear. Because of these factors, many new-car dealers refuse to replace disc pads without cutting the discs. In the interest of avoiding customer complaints, I think the policy makes some sense. Independent shops tend to be a lot more flexible though, and often do not object to installing new pads for use with scored discs.

How Much Disc Cutting Is Too Much? Excessive cutting of brake discs is very common. It is also very dangerous. When a disc is machined too much, it is too thin to properly dissipate heat. This could lead to fracturing and an accident. If your mechanic tells you that your car's brake discs need cutting, insist that he measure the final thickness of the discs. He should record the measurements on the repair order. If he gives you a hassle about doing this, it could be because he doesn't know how to read a micrometer or doesn't own one, in which case he shouldn't be doing brake work to begin with.

If only one of the front discs is too thin after machining to safely use it, it's a good idea to replace both discs with new ones. The metallurgical properties of replacement discs can differ somewhat from the originals, and you shouldn't have a mismatched set on your car.

You can generally expect competent disc machining at new-car dealers and the larger chain service centers. These facilities are sensitive to potential lawsuits and usually do brake work cautiously and conservatively. I've noticed that some smaller independent shops are more apt to throw caution to the wind. Over the years, I've seen some incredible butcher jobs come out of these places as far as brake work is concerned. The price can be low, but so can the quality. For the sake of your own safety, make sure you are doing business with a competent brake mechanic, and don't make price your overriding concern.

Some Other Good Reasons Not to Machine Brake Discs. In an effort to reduce weight, auto manufacturers have been using lighter and lighter brake discs. When these discs are cut, there is less metal available to dissipate heat. This results in shorter life of replacement brake pads. This is the main reason why replacement pads never seem to last as long as the originals. Additionally, machined discs are more likely to warp after vigorous braking.

If the thickness of your car's brake discs is close to the minimum limit, it is best to install a set of new discs. This will be a lot more expensive than machining the old ones, but it will be a more reliable repair.

► The Brake Fluid

Brake fluid is one of the most neglected and improperly serviced components of any car's hydraulic brake system. If you plan to get 100,000 miles of driving out of your car, you should ask your mechanic to drain the brake fluid and flush the hydraulic brake lines after the first five years or 50,000 miles, whichever comes first, or on the first occasion when routine brake work is done.

I don't recall ever seeing an automobile owner's manual that specified a brake fluid change at a particular interval.

Most auto service manuals just suggest draining and flushing the brake system if evidence of fluid contamination or deterioration is observed. The fact is, however, that contamination and fluid deterioration is inevitable and usually unnoticeable. And certainly by the time it is noticeable, damage has already occurred.

It is well known that brake fluid is exceptionally *hygroscopic*, that is, it absorbs moisture from the atmosphere. What is not so commonly known is that the fluid can absorb moisture even though the master cylinder is kept closed. Flexible brake hoses have micro-porous openings that will not cause external leaks, but can admit some atmospheric moisture that slowly contaminates the brake fluid. The rubber seals in front brake calipers and rear-wheel cylinders can also allow moisture to pass through to the fluid.

Once contaminated by moisture, the brake fluid begins to break down. It's ability to prevent corrosion is reduced along with its boiling point and lubricating properties. Consequently, wheel cylinders and brake calipers can slowly corrode, eventually leading to fluid leaks, or seizure of the parts and "dragging" brakes, that is, brakes that stay partially applied even though you take your foot off the brake pedal. A lowered boiling point can result in a serious loss of braking power during repeated quick stops or prolonged use descending steep grades.

These problems are severe enough for the automotive industry to have sought out nonhygroscopic alternatives to conventional brake fluid. One solution has been silicone-based fluids that do not absorb water, but do have some drawbacks, so it's not likely that your car's manufacturer recommends them. But this does not mean you can't take other measures to prolong the life of your car's hydraulic brake system.

I have already mentioned draining the fluid and flushing the brake lines. This is an easy job for a mechanic to do, especially when your car is in for routine brake service. In less than ten minutes of additional time, the hydraulic system can be purged and fresh brake fluid added. The entire operation shouldn't add more than $15 to your bill. The benefit comes later on, when you don't have to spend hundreds of dollars on new calipers and wheel cylinders.

► *Sliding Caliper Support Brackets*

Sloppy mechanics frequently overlook the need to clean sliding caliper support brackets when they perform disc brake work. This oversight typically results in uneven braking and premature wearing out of the new brake pads.

A sliding caliper disc brake, found on many car lines, is characterized by the use of a single-piston caliper that moves freely (slides) from side to side on its fixed, or unmovable, support bracket (Figure 7). A so-called floating caliper operates on a similar principle, but slides on guide pins affixed to the support bracket. When the brakes are applied, the expansion of the caliper piston toward the disc forces one pad against the disc while the caliper jaws pull the opposing pad into the disc. For this type of brake

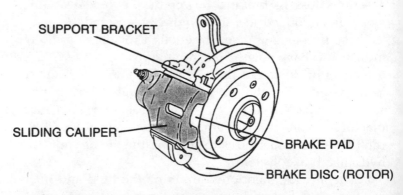

SUPPORT BRACKET

SLIDING CALIPER

BRAKE PAD

BRAKE DISC (ROTOR)

Figure 7. Sliding caliper disc brakes are characterized by a single-piston caliper that slides laterally on a fixed support bracket.

to work correctly, the caliper must float freely on the support bracket, and the brake pads must also move freely.

Figure 8 shows a disassembled view of a typical sliding caliper including the fixed support bracket, the caliper, and the brake pads. You will note from the illustration that certain surfaces of the caliper and the support bracket must be clean. During prolonged use, after exposure to moisture and road salt, these surfaces rust and corrode. They should be thoroughly cleaned with a wire brush and coated with a suitable brake lubricant. If this is not done, the caliper will not float freely on the bracket and the new brake pads may not apply and release evenly.

Failure to adequately clean these surfaces is a common mistake made by sloppy or poorly trained mechanics. I've seen dozens of cases where rusted or corroded calipers and support brackets were reassembled by beating them into place with a hammer. This sort of brute force incompetence usually occurs at some independent repair shops and small garages that employ cheap labor.

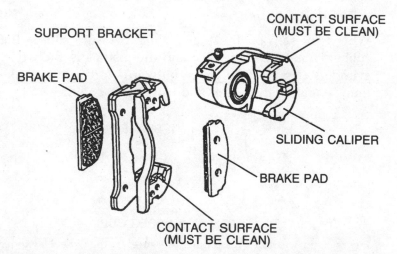

Figure 8. On a sliding caliper disc brake, the contact surfaces of the support bracket and the caliper must be clean and free of rust and corrosion. Failure to clean these surfaces during a brake overhaul is a common mistake made by sloppy mechanics.

Rarely will a new-car dealership or major chain service center produce horrendous work of this nature. But dealerships usually charge more for repairs, a fact not too appealing to bargain hunters. You would be wise, however, not to make price your main concern with this kind of brake work, because a seemingly small error such as not cleaning the hardware properly will usually cause the new pads to fail after a few thousand miles.

Drum Brake Rip-offs

On most late-model cars, drum brakes are only used on the rear wheels. Mechanics servicing drum brakes frequently gyp consumers in the following ways:

- ► By replacing wheel cylinders unnecessarily
- ► By machining rear brake drums unnecessarily
- ► By excessively machining rear brake drums

► The Wheel Cylinders

When you step on the brake, fluid pressure causes the rubber cups (movable seals) and the pistons in the wheel cylinders (Figure 9) to move outward, forcing the brake linings against the drum and slowing it down.

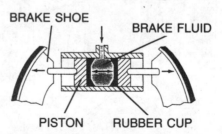

Figure 9. In a drum brake fluid pressure in the wheel cylinder forces the pistons out, thereby moving the brake linings (shoes) into contact with the drum. The rubber cups seal the brake fluid in the wheel cylinder.

The outside of a wheel cylinder is surrounded by a rubber boot that helps keep out dirt and water. Some minor brake fluid seepage can accumulate beneath the boot leaving a damp stain (Figure 10) on the wheel cylinder. This is normal and does not represent a problem.

RUBBER BOOT   RUBBER BOOT

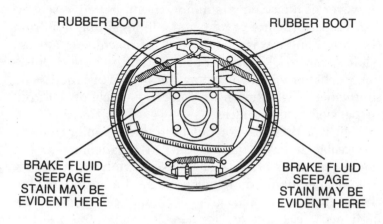

BRAKE FLUID   BRAKE FLUID
SEEPAGE   SEEPAGE
STAIN MAY BE   STAIN MAY BE
EVIDENT HERE   EVIDENT HERE

Figure 10. The outside of a wheel cylinder is surrounded by a rubber boot. Some minor seepage can accumulate beneath the boot, leaving a stain on the wheel cylinder. This is a normal condition.

Some unscrupulous mechanics will point to this stain as evidence of wheel cylinder leakage and convince an unwary customer that a new wheel cylinder is required when in fact it is not. If the boot is pulled away from the wheel cylinder and fluid drips out, that constitutes an unacceptable leak requiring rebuilding or replacement of the wheel cylinder.

If your car does have one or more leaking wheel cylinders, you are generally better off asking for new ones than having the old cylinders rebuilt. Whether or not a wheel cylinder can be successfully reconditioned is a judgment call that many mechanics are incapable of making correctly. Go with new parts to be on the safe side.

► *The Drums and Linings*

As is the case with discs, brake drums are often unnecessarily machined. If a drum's friction surface is
smooth, machining generally is not necessary. Scoring, as
previously described for discs, justifies cutting a drum.
However, if the scoring is minor, it will not adversely affect the performance of new brake linings. But, if a drum
is out of round ("warped"), it *must* be machined. You can
tell if a rear brake drum is out of round if you feel pulsation or chatter when you apply the brakes but there is no
simultaneous vibration in the steering wheel or the front
suspension of the vehicle.

Even if a drum is not out of round, it might not be
serviceable if it has blue spots on its friction surface.
These blue spots are caused by excessive heating and result in alterations in the drum's hardness and friction
characteristics. In some cases machining can cut away the
hardened areas, but replacement is usually the best bet.

It is desirable to avoid machining rear brake drums whenever possible. Drums have a greater tendency to "warp"
than discs. Cutting away metal from the inside of the drum
weakens it and increases this tendency, and along with it the
likelihood that additional cutting will be necessary later on.

Another reason to avoid cutting a brake drum is that
new linings will not properly fit the machined drum.
When a drum is cut, its inside radius is increased. However, the radius of the linings is not. Consequently, the
new linings will initially achieve only partial contact with
the drum (Figure 11), sometimes causing overheating and
damage to the lining and drum.

In the past, this was prevented by a procedure called
radius grinding, also commonly referred to as arc grinding.
Radius grinding entailed using a special machine to grind
off some of the new brake lining to a radius matching that
of the machined drum (Figure 11). Because of recent dis-

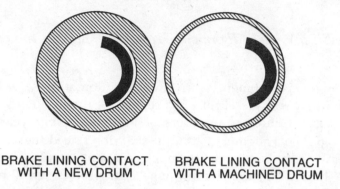

**BRAKE LINING CONTACT
WITH A NEW DRUM**

**BRAKE LINING CONTACT
WITH A MACHINED DRUM**

Figure 11. When brakes are new the radius of the linings matches the radius of the drums. Consequently, the entire lining is in contact with the drum when the brakes are applied. When a drum is machined, its radius increases, resulting in only partial contact of the lining with the drum. It is best to avoid machining brake drums unless absolutely necessary to restore a good friction surface.

coveries about the adverse health effects of asbestos, radius grinding is rarely done anymore. The procedure throws off a lot of dangerous asbestos dust from the linings as they are ground.

If it is absolutely necessary for your mechanic to machine your car's brake drums, ask him to record on your repair order the final drum diameter after machining and the manufacturer's maximum recommended diameter. It is not uncommon for mechanics to cut drums dangerously thin. Insisting that the machining specifications be made available to you will go a long way in motivating your mechanic to do the best and safest possible brake job on your car.

As a rule of thumb, no brake drum should be cut more than .060″ greater than its original diameter. Also, the diameters of the two rear drums should be within .010″ of each other to ensure equal rear-braking action.

Wheel Alignment, Balancing, and Front Suspension Repairs

Will a Wheel Alignment Fix a "Shimmy" in the Front End?

Wheel alignment is an area of automotive service so fraught with deceitful practices that it might qualify as a racket. Countless numbers of motorists every year are sold wheel alignments on cars that don't need them. Typically, the customer complains about a vibration or "shimmy" in the steering wheel at speeds over 40 miles per hour. A shop manager or mechanic leads the customer to believe that an alignment and wheel balancing will correct the problem. In fact, while the wheel balancing might fix the problem, the alignment is certainly a waste of money. Wheel alignment can correct certain kinds of handling difficulties and tire wear, but it will not rectify vibration problems.

Most cases of steering-wheel vibration and front-end shimmy are caused by improper wheel/tire balance or out-of-round tires. You can tell if a tire is out-of-round by raising it off the ground with a jack. Make sure the vehicle is adequately supported so that there is no danger that it might slip off the jack. Hold a pencil across the front of the tire about an eighth of an inch away from the tread. Then spin the tire and observe whether or not it seems to move in and out toward the pencil. If it appears to move more than one-eighth of an inch, it may have excessive "radial runout," a more technical way to describe an out-of-round condition. If the wheel on which the tire is mounted is somewhat out-of-round, sometimes repositioning the tire on the wheel and rebalancing the wheel and tire assembly will correct the steering wheel vibration. In other cases the only cure is a new tire.

More likely than an out-of-round tire is one that is simply not properly balanced. Left this way over thousands of miles of driving, the tire will wear unevenly, displaying scalloped depressions or "cups" on the tread (Figure 12). If these depressions get deep enough, the tire becomes so noisy that it can sound as though a wheel bearing were failing.

It is not uncommon for new cars to roll off the assembly line with improperly balanced tires. If you feel a steering-wheel vibration in a new car, make sure your dealer does a wheel-balance check before cups begin to form in the tire tread. On older cars, you should always suspect incorrect wheel/tire balance as the cause of vibration and get this tended to before trying new shock absorbers or major front-suspension repairs. A lot of mechanics mistakenly or deceitfully try to sell their customers new ball

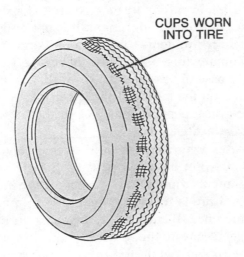

CUPS WORN
INTO TIRE

Figure 12. Cups (depressions) worn into a tire usually result from many miles of driving with the tire improperly balanced. Sometimes, cupped tires are caused by bad shock absorbers or worn suspension components, including defective MacPherson struts. These problems are infrequent compared to tire imbalance.

joints and shock absorbers, along with a wheel balance and front-end alignment as a packaged deal to fix a steering-wheel vibration. Unless you trust your mechanic implicitly, just go for the wheel balancing and get a second opinion about the need for additional work.

How to Tell That Your Car Needs a Wheel Alignment

Unlike wheel/tire imbalance that causes front-end vibration, a wheel alignment problem manifests itself by way of drifting or pulling to one side while driving on a flat surface, and/or abnormal tire wear. Whether or not you notice the tire wear depends on how far your vehicle has been driven with the wheels misaligned.

If your car pulls to one side but the front tires appear to be wearing evenly, you may be able to spare yourself the expense of a wheel alignment. It is not unusual for certain internal tire problems to cause a pull or a drift to one side. To eliminate this possibility, have the two front wheel and tire assemblies interchanged, that is, install the right front tire on the left, and the left front tire on the right. If the pull disappears or changes to the opposite direction, you have a tire problem.

In cases where uneven tire wear is evident, you can easily interpret the wear patterns to determine what kind of alignment trouble your car has. If the inside or outside edge of a tire is uniformly worn down around the entire circumference (Figure 13), it indicates an incorrect *camber* setting. Wear on the outside edge is due to excessive *positive* camber, while too much *negative* camber accounts for wear on the inside edge. Either way, resetting camber can be a time-consuming process on many cars, so expect to pay for a complete wheel alignment to restore proper front-end geometry.

If the edges of the tire tread are feathered (Figure 13)

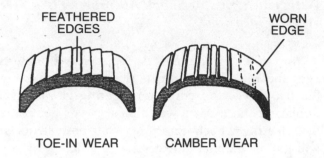

Figure 13. Tire wear due to incorrect toe-in is characterized by feathering at the edges of the tread. Excessive wear on one side of the tire around its entire circumference is due to improper camber. A wheel alignment is usually all that is needed to prevent a new set of tires from wearing out the same way.

across the face of the tire, a *toe-in* problem is indicated. Correcting improper toe-in is easier than adjusting camber and should cost less than a complete wheel alignment. When your car is on the alignment rack for a toe-in adjustment, your mechanic can check camber and caster (I'll talk more about caster in a second) without any big additional effort. If they are okay, you shouldn't have to pay the same amount to simply *check* these settings as you would if an actual adjustment were performed.

Now, getting back to the matter of *caster*—this is an alignment angle that will make your car pull to the left or the right if the adjustment is incorrect. However, improperly adjusted caster will not cause uneven tire wear as is the case with toe-in and camber. Caster adjustments are included in the price of a complete wheel alignment.

Many cars built in the 1980s have adjustable rear-suspension geometry. On these cars, a rear-wheel alignment could be required from time to time. The tire wear patterns are the same as those discussed in connection with misaligned front wheels.

Will New Struts or Shock Absorbers Fix a Steering-Wheel Vibration?

Next to wheel alignments, replacement of shock absorbers and MacPherson struts (Figure 14) ranks highest on the list of voodoo cures for steering-vibration ailments. Replacing these parts will almost never get rid of abnormal steering-wheel vibration. What new struts or shocks will do is eliminate excessive bouncing of a car and "wheel hop" when going over bumps.

To verify that your car needs new front struts or shocks, lean on each side of the front bumper and bounce the car up and down a few times and release it. If the car continues to bounce more than once before it stops, new shocks or struts are probably required. The same test can be done at the rear bumper.

If defective struts are indicated, it is sometimes possible to replace just the worn out damper cartridges (shock ab-

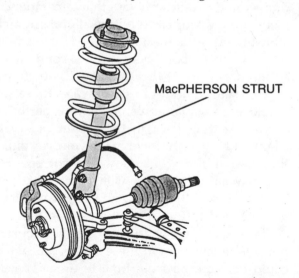

MacPHERSON STRUT

Figure 14. In a MacPherson strut front suspension, the shock absorbers are located inside the strut assemblies.

sorbing mechanism inside the strut) instead of the entire strut. For those cars that don't have replaceable cartridges, there are aftermarket struts available that come equipped with replaceable units, making subsequent strut service less expensive.

Automatic Transmission Repairs

The Metal Particles in the Oil Pan Scam

A favorite scam of the automatic transmission repair business involves baiting a customer into the shop for an amazingly low-priced fluid and filter change, band adjustment, and inspection service with the hope of selling far more expensive and often unnecessary work.

When the transmission oil pan is removed to access the filter, the customer is shown metal particles accumulated at the bottom of the pan. The allegation is made that these particles indicate very serious internal damage that must be fixed right away. If you fall for the scam, you're in for a costly transmission overhaul that your car probably doesn't need. You see, all automatic transmissions accumulate some metal particles in the oil pan—it's perfectly normal. So, if you are given this sales pitch, get your transmission put back together again fast and make a quick exit before you get fleeced.

Transmission shops often are the targets of sting operations run by television journalists and newspaper reporters. The purpose of the sting operation is to expose fraudulent practices. Typically, a car is rigged to create a shift problem; usually the throttle cable is deliberately maladjusted to delay upshift speeds. The car is brought to several transmission shops to test the honesty of each shop—that is, which shops will do the required inexpensive cable adjustment and which shops will try to sell an unnecessary major overhaul?

Inevitably, some shops prove to be quite honest, and others try the unethical approach. Even major shops such as AAMCO get "caught" in these sting operations from time to time. However, you should not assume that because one or two shops act dishonestly they are all dishonest. The owners of AAMCO, Lee Myles, and other major transmission shops are independent franchisees. How they treat some of their customers is not under direct control of the parent corporation or franchisor. It's similar to a situation where a car dealer goes to jail for rolling back odometers on used cars. If a Honda or Chevy dealer is caught doing this, it certainly doesn't mean Honda Motor Company or General Motors is in any way culpable.

Engine Service

Bogus Valve Adjustments

Some domestic cars and many imported models have engines that require periodic valve adjustments. If the valve clearances are excessive, you hear an annoying tapping and clattering under the hood. Clearances that are too narrow are even worse, since "tight" valves will be quiet but will also burn out prematurely.

Many valve adjustments that motorists pay for are never really done. Often, mechanics are so brazen in the way they chisel their customers that they don't even bother to remove the valve cover (Figure 15), a necessary preliminary step to access the adjustment mechanism. If you have any doubts about the honesty of the shop you are doing business with, you can put a mark on a fastener on the valve cover to make sure that a mechanic at least went through the motions of removing the cover.

Put a small dab of paint or colored nail polish on one of the nuts or bolts (Figure 15) that fasten the valve cover to the cylinder head. The paint must touch the nut or bolt and a portion of the valve cover itself. Pick an inconspicuous location and make the dab of paint very small so as not to advertise your actions. After the work is done, if the paint has not been disturbed, you know that the hardware was not removed, so the valve adjustment could not have been done. In that case, get your money back and find another shop.

The Phony Cooling System Flush

A car's cooling system should be drained and flushed every few years. Left in the engine too long, antifreeze

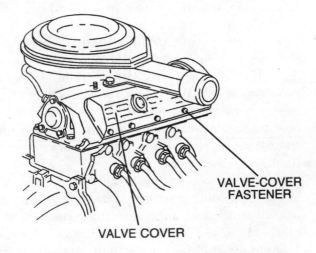

VALVE-COVER
FASTENER

VALVE COVER

Figure 15. Motorists are frequently charged for valve adjustments that are not really done. To adjust the valves, the valve cover on the engine must be removed. Crooked mechanics don't even go through the motions of removing the valve cover. A dab of paint put on the base of one of the valve-cover fasteners in an inconspicuous location can tip you off if the cover was not removed.

loses its rust-inhibiting properties and its ability to prevent corrosion. This leads to a clogged radiator and greater likelihood of overheating in hot weather. After several years, the engine can develop serious coolant leaks due to insufficient rust inhibition. Also, the heater core can clog, thereby reducing its efficiency and its ability to heat the car's interior.

Many repair shops advertise cooling system maintenance, which they claim includes draining and flushing the cooling system and adding fresh antifreeze. Almost invariably, they do not do what their advertisements claim. What they purport to be a cooling system flush usually amounts to no more than draining the radiator and adding some antifreeze. This is completely unsatisfactory because only 40 or 50 percent of the total coolant is in the radiator; the rest is in the engine block, heater core, cooling system hoses, and coolant expansion reservoir.

In a cooling system with a 10-quart capacity, more than 5 quarts of deteriorated antifreeze/water mixture can be left behind if only the radiator is drained. This creates two problems. First, the corrosion protection offered by the fresh antifreeze is reduced by the presence of the worn-out residual mixture. Second, the addition of fresh antifreeze may increase the percentage of antifreeze to a level harmful to the engine.

Mechanics generally add new antifreeze in proportion to the total cooling system capacity to create a 50-50 mixture of water and antifreeze. In a 10-quart system, your mechanic would typically drain the radiator and then add 5 quarts of antifreeze expecting to produce a 50-50 mixture. Unfortunately, this doesn't take into account the residual water/antifreeze mixture left in the engine block, heater core, etc. Consequently, the percentage of antifreeze could wind up a lot higher than 50 percent of the total coolant capacity. An excessively high concentration of antifreeze can cause problems. Studies have shown that using greater than 50 percent antifreeze can lead to the formation of deposits in certain areas of the engine, thereby reducing thermal conductivity. Put simply, this means some spots inside the engine can overheat.

Considering how important it is for your car's cooling system to be properly serviced, you should ask your mechanic to clarify how he normally performs a cooling system flush before you let him do the job. If he just intends to drain the radiator, you should advise him that you want the engine block drained too and the entire system *back-flushed*. Back-flushing is a procedure that entails using clean water to pump all of the coolant out of the cooling system and continuing the process until the water runs clear. If your mechanic gives you a line about how tough it is to back-flush a cooling system, you might remind him that "do-it-yourself" back-flush kits are sold in department stores. If the job is easy enough for a novice to handle, it shouldn't be too difficult for a skilled mechanic.

Air-Conditioner Service

The Bubbles-in-the-Sight-Glass Scam. Every spring, repair shops advertise air conditioner service specials. For a flat fee, your car's air conditioning system will be checked out and R12 refrigerant will be added as needed, at an extra cost for the refrigerant.

As it turns out, this ridiculously overpriced refrigerant is almost always needed, as indicated by bubbles and foam in the system's sight glass. At least that's what some mechanics claim. Most consumers will not question the decision to add refrigerant since they are shown by their mechanic that the bubbles and foam disappear after addition of the extra refrigerant.

Actually, some foam in the sight glass is normal at low

engine rpms. Adding additional refrigerant, also referred to as "charging the system," can do more harm than good. Here's why. An automotive air conditioning system will function at 90 percent of its capacity if it is 50 percent *undercharged*. It will only function at 50 percent of its capacity if it is just 10 percent *overcharged*. That's why so many motorists complain that their air conditioners don't seem to run as cold as they used to after they have been serviced.

Another reason for a reduction in cooling performance is related to improper air conditioner service procedure used by many auto mechanics. If an air conditioner is inoperative, chances are its refrigerant has been lost due to a leak. Depending on the location and size of the leak, air and moisture can enter the system after all the refrigerant has leaked out. If a mechanic simply adds more refrigerant, the air conditioner may work, but at greatly reduced efficiency due to the presence of air and excessive moisture.

The correct procedure entails *evacuating* the system with a special vacuum pump. This removes any air present and boils off moisture. More often than not, mechanics don't bother doing this. The result is an air conditioner that doesn't cool as well as it should, or occasionally stops working completely because of moisture which forms ice crystals that block the expansion valve.

As a rule of thumb, you should insist that your car's air conditioner be thoroughly evacuated any time it has lost all its refrigerant or whenever the system is opened up for repairs, such as replacement of cracked tubing or hoses.

▼ ▼ ▼

Index

Index

▼ ▼ ▼

About the Author

Sal Fariello has nearly twenty years of involvement with the automotive industry. Working for auto manufacturers, he has been a regional service manager with Volvo of America Corporation and with Alfa Romeo, Inc. Before that, he was a service manager with two Ford dealerships, a Datsun dealership, and a large independent foreign-car repair shop. He has also been an assistant service manager with a Chrysler dealership.

Sal's experience with automotive service has not been limited to management positions. His hands-on, practical background includes having worked as a head mechanic in Chrysler and Datsun dealerships, and a class A technician in Volvo, Fiat, Mercedes-Benz, and Jaguar dealerships.

Sal has also written extensively about automobile repair as well as a variety of technology-oriented subjects. He has authored articles that have appeared in the automotive trade press, and has written complete automotive maintenance and repair manuals for the United States Army. He has also written dozens of magazine articles dealing with state-of-the-art electronics technology. Consequently, Sal is intimately familiar with microcomputer applications in modern automobiles.

Frequently, attorneys call on Sal for help as a consultant and expert witness in automotive-accident and product-liability cases. However, the majority of his time is presently occupied as president of a firm that specializes in the development of technical educational materials for industrial clients.